Globalization and World Society

Globalization and World Society

Tony Spybey

Polity Press

Copyright © Tony Spybey 1996

The right of Tony Spybey to be identified as author of this work has been
asserted in accordance with the Copyright, Designs and Patents Act 1988.

First published in 1996 by Polity Press in association with Blackwell Publishers
Ltd.

2 4 6 8 9 10 7 5 3 1

Editorial office:
Polity Press
65 Bridge Street
Cambridge CB2 1UR, UK

Marketing and production:
Blackwell Publishers Ltd
108 Cowley Road
Oxford OX4 1JF, UK

Blackwell Publishers Inc.
238 Main Street
Cambridge, MA 02142, USA

ISBN 0–7456–1158–3
ISBN 0–7456–1159–1 (pbk)

A CIP catalogue record for this book is available from the British Library and
the Library of Congress.

Typeset in 10.5 on 12.5 pt Times
by Best-set Typesetter Ltd., Hong Kong
Printed in Great Britain by Hartnolls Ltd, Bodmin, Cornwall

This book is printed on acid-free paper.

Contents

vi *Contents*

Tables

Acknowledgements

I should like to thank Tony Giddens for his encouragement and for his customary incisively helpful comments on drafts of the manuscript. Thanks are also due to Dave Dawson, Eric Harrison, Colin Rallings and Michael Thrasher who are all colleagues at Plymouth. Responsibility for what appears in the final version of course remains entirely with me.

The author and publishers would like to thank *Fortune International* for information used in the compilation of Tables 5 and 6.

They have made every effort to trace all copyright holders. If any has been inadvertently overlooked, they will be pleased to make the necessary arrangements at the first opportunity.

Preface

In a previous book, *Social Change, Development and Dependency* (1992), I set out a sociological approach to the rise of the West, the effects of this on other parts of the world and the outcome in the twentieth century. This was intended to address a need that I perceived for more substantive time and space dimensions in the study of social development. Running through all twentieth-century outcomes of the rise of the West, however, is the concept of globalization. Therefore I now present this, complementary, volume on the social processes of globalization and the notion of world society.

In chapter 1 the rise of the West is examined once again but this time specifically in terms of the growth of a European world view effective enough to lead to the cultural, political and economic domination of the globe. It was Europeans who first acquired a 'scientific' outward-looking perspective which contrasted with the mystical and inward-looking world views of other civilizations. It proved to be convincing enough to set in motion successful oceanic exploration and the global influence that followed from that. In short, the Earth was objectified, measured and owned. In the longer term, however, it has been the sheer pervasiveness of 'Western' cultural influence that most starkly contrasts with other civilizations' prior attempts at territorial conquest. The rise of the West is also distinct in being the achievement of a system of independent states rather than a singular hierarchical empire. The spread of a 'rational' view of the world and the development of an effective and enduring state system are both significant indications of what we regard as 'modernization' in Western society.

During the first half of the twentieth century the achievements of Western civilization reached unprecedented levels in material terms. The focus of this was the development of 'consumer society' in the USA, a nation-state established in the first place with the central ideal of putting New World opportunity in the place of European privilege. An integral part of this social project was the extension of mass participation in politics and economics as a matter of principle. Chapter 2, therefore, addresses the creation of a mass production, mass communication and mass consumption society in the USA, from where the rest of the world has derived images of attractive new products and associated lifestyles. Impressions of the 'American dream' were carried in the form of cultural flows along global pathways of communication created as part of the rise of the West. Popular culture of American origin began to be spread through the media of cinema, broadcasting and recorded music during the early decades of the twentieth century. Ironically, this was at approximately the same time that reports of the decline of the West began to appear. These resulted largely from the carnage and futility of the First World War, a war of European origin, but one subsequently spreading to many parts of the world and fought with products of Western industrialization. It was also the occasion of the USA's first major logistical incursion into Europe as an independent power; a perceived 'Americanization' of the world began to draw criticism too.

The media of popular culture were developed in the USA, but they became the hallmarks of a broader twentieth-century Western culture which constituted a new phase in the process of globalization. The capacity of modern Western culture to erode other cultures, including surviving aspects of traditional European culture, is testimony to the continuing progress of Western modernization. There may be aesthetic and conceptual problems in tracing Western society's 'civilizing process' and 'Enlightenment project' through to these twentieth-century developments in mass consumption, but the emancipatory principles which characterize Western modernization did emerge in new forms. The 'American dream' of enhanced materialistic lifestyles is a form of economic emancipation which during the twentieth century has accompanied the political and social emancipation begun in the nineteenth century.

Greater in its overall effects than either the rise of the West or the subsequent 'Americanization' of the world, however, is the continuing reproduction of globalized social institutions. This has affected the lives of virtually the entire population of the planet during the closing decades of the twentieth century. It constitutes the full meaning of the word 'globalization'. The reproduction of global culture by people everywhere may be seen as the reflexive effect of global cultural flows. The concept of world society, therefore, is intended to address the extent to which people, consciously and subconsciously in their regular social practices, have reference to patterns of behaviour and material resources derived from global cultural flows. The premise is that, through such influence, virtually the whole world has acquired aspirations to standards of living and lifestyles that have roots in Western culture. Furthermore, this premise holds despite the fact that the majority of people in the world still lack the means adequately to fulfil such aspirations.

The central purpose of this book, then, is to examine the concept of globalization in terms of overarching connections through which routine or institutionalized aspects of social life have become globally linked. This approach embraces structural characteristics of global cultural homogeneity, globalized processes of cultural reproduction and, most important of all, the outcomes to these as they affect the day-to-day lives of people everywhere. Lifestyle aspirations and associated patterns of behaviour are taken to be indications of global culture and, for purposes of conceptual analysis, I have divided up global institutions into separate dimensions of citizenship and polity, production/consumption and economy, knowledge and communication, world order and the military, and social movements. Such dimensions overlap in practice, but for purposes of analysis each is addressed here in a separate chapter. In each case the relationship between the individual and the global is emphasized.

Chapter 3 is devoted to the global polity and attention is particularly focused on the Western model of the nation-state and the ubiquity of this form in the global nation-state system. The surface area of the planet is divided up into the territories of nation-states and it is through this spatial arrangement that 'international relations' are conducted. In the twentieth century people derive a considerable part of their identity from their affiliation as citizens of nation-states and indeed in the absence of this affiliation the role of the stateless person is extremely problematic. The most striking aspect of the global polity is the ubiquity of the nation-state model, even taking into account those cases where its existence is corrupted or misused. Ideals of citizenship and citizenship rights have been derived from conceptions of civilization, enlightenment and modernization in Western society and it is through the Western model of the nation-state that they are maintained. Testimony to this is provided by the United Nations' Declaration of Human Rights which enshrines these ideals in legal form. Such ideals became globalized as a 'standard of civilization' when the influence of Western civilization became virtually universal at the end of the nineteenth century. Today, unsatisfactory examples of the nation-state are identified by the absence or scarcity of citizenship rights and yet in virtually all cases the major institutions of government, administration, judiciary and forces of coercion are maintained in a recognizable, if often corrupted, form.

Chapter 4 addresses processes of integration in the global economy and the international division of labour. Europeans became involved in an international division of labour of their own making as soon as they began to depend on the produce of overseas trade and colonial enterprise. The Industrial Revolution was a revolution in production techniques which intensified the demand for the supply of goods internationally. During the twentieth century industrialized mass production has been developed into an integrated system involving a broader-based and more widespread international division of labour. There is also a growing incidence of relocation and global distribution in manufacturing sites. In the late twentieth century this process has developed to the extent that there exist what amount to globalized production lines. These have a dual effect, either involving more and more people around the world as producers and consumers in some way, or highlighting the exclusion of people from substantive participation in the global economy, despite the fact that the global communication system ensures that virtually everyone is informed of the possibilities.

Chapter 5 looks at global communications and especially at the 'electronic revolution' and the so-called 'information super-highway' during the closing decade of the twentieth century. As early as the Renaissance, the widespread use of the printing press began to revolutionize the exchange of knowledge. During the Industrial Revolution the railways made possible the routine dissemination of information through the delivery of daily national newspapers. The development of electronics, however, has enabled information to be sent along wires and through the airwaves without the accompaniment of human messengers. Satellite transmissions and optical fibre cabling have added to this by hugely extending the capacity to supply continuous and instantaneous information. The potential range of sources is truly global but in practice authority over the process and the allocation of its benefits is determined through global political and economic institutions.

Chapter 6 addresses world order and the globalization of military institutions. Industrialization provided the capacity for the mass production of weapons and for the development of 'industrialized warfare'. This involves not just participants on the battlefield but also the general population in a form that has been alternatively referred to as 'total warfare'. The industrialization of armaments production has made the capacity for waging war more widely available and this has impinged upon the authority of the nation-state, especially in terms of its 'monopoly of the legitimate means of violence'. The modern state was established largely through the concentration of administrative capacity and military force, since these gave it the means to secure and maintain authority. But, with the mass production of armaments, forces in opposition to the nation-state have frequently obtained access to sophisticated weaponry too. People are drawn into this situation as members of the armed forces of nation-states – 'the security forces' – or, alternatively, as guerrillas or freedom fighters – 'terrorists'. An additional factor to be addressed is the removal of the traditional gender distinction in the membership of either group.

Chapter 7 is directed at the rather different topic of global social movements. These movements in fact question some of the effects of globalization but at the same time derive benefits from flows of global culture in order to propagate their message. There are forms of social protest which have been organized formally, such as Amnesty International against militarism and authoritarian government, or Friends of the Earth and Greenpeace against environmental pollution. But increasingly global movements operate without formal organization through the exchange of information, role models and modes of operation facilitated by the global communication system. The feminist movement is a good example of this. Such exchanges are apparently sufficient to engage a much wider range of people in protest and negotiation with the official agencies of polity and economy.

This book concludes with an appraisal of the relationship between the individual and the global in the light of the pervasive global cultural influences described in the various chapters and briefly referred to above. Towards the end of the twentieth century the individual, as never before, is subject to a continuous array of global influences. But the important factor is the way in which people reproduce social institutions in the light of these pervasive global models. This alone reveals the true meaning of globalization, which is essentially a reflexive process involving both global cultural inputs and local acts of reproduction. Globalization can only exist when, on a global scale, people take up and reproduce social institutions in their local milieu. The final chapter pursues this 'interpenetration' of global and local influences and includes assessments of the various conceptual approaches to globalization.

Introduction

According to Clive Gamble (1994) the first indication of globalization is the near global distribution of homo sapiens. Humans are the only species with such widespread distribution on the planet and Gamble argues that this is not the result of random processes but of intention and planning, characteristics that are clearly part of the human condition. However, this only refers to the distribution of the human species on the planet. A different definition of the origins of globalization is in terms of the aftermath of the voyages of Christopher Columbus in 1492 and Vasco da Gama in 1497–8, when Europeans began to exert an influence on the rest of the world and implant their cultural institutions on all continents. The acquisition of a world view by Europeans produced as its long-term outcome the world's first truly global culture.

The development of a twentieth-century global culture has, however, been different because it has consisted of trends which, more than anything which went before, have involved, in some way or other, virtually everyone on the planet. By the last decade of the twentieth century it has become almost impossible to avoid the influences of the nation-state system, the global economy, the global communication system and the world military order. The USA played a significant part in the development of global dimensions to social institutions through the propagation of the 'mass participation society' with institutions open to all. In the development of an independent New World, the systems of privilege inherent in traditional European society were superseded. Instead the characteristically

American ideal of enterprise was dedicated in principle to the extending of broad new opportunities. In a political sense the principle of mass participation was established with the Declaration of Independence, but an economic dimension was added with the twentieth-century 'American dream' of rising living standards through large-scale consumption. The principle of mass consumption through mass production originated during the early decades of this century largely from the pioneering influences of Frederick Winslow Taylor in 'scientific management' and Henry Ford in the development of assembly-line manufacturing. 'Taylorism' and 'Fordism' each had a major input into the organization of production and provided a *modus operandi* for fast-growing American companies. Some of these have developed into the giant transnational corporations of the late twentieth century.

In these terms mass participation through mass production involves the principle of producing for everyone at a price that anyone can pay. The outcome is mass consumption, to which is added the 'lubrication' of mass communication. The direct advertising of products and the transmission of idealized images of consumer culture have been carried through the media of broadcasting, cinema, popular music and, ultimately, television. All of these were developed on a large scale in the USA. Mass production, mass communication and mass consumption might be seen as a kind of trinity of 'high modernity', the materialistic culmination of the 'Enlightenment project' in the sense that they provided opportunities for people to harness science and technology and improve their standard of living. In these terms the propagation of the American dream was a process of emancipation, but of course it is not to be confused with the achievement of equality. The American model of society tends to be one of rugged individualism and the eschewing of state-sponsored enterprise. Equality of opportunity is held to be an overriding principle, but the society is competitive and equality of outcomes is not the goal. In terms of globalization this model, with its emancipatory effects and inequalities, was carried along global channels of cultural flow created with the rise of the West and its impact upon the rest of the world. The outcome during the twentieth century has been a world increasingly globalized and, in many people's eyes, 'Americanized'.

Global dimensions for this twentieth-century model of social development may be defined in terms of polity, economy, communication and world order. In what may be regarded as the global polity, the Western model of the nation-state has been adopted throughout the world, and the resulting nation-state system now involves the operation of clearly defined procedures of international relations. The nation-state model consists in principle of representative government, bureaucratic administration, independent judiciary and monopoly of the legitimate means of violence. The global nation-state system was extended during the mid-twentieth century as European colonialism was brought to an end and many new 'emergent nations' were created. The United Nations had fifty member states at its foundation in 1945 but now has more than 200. People in Africa, Asia and Latin America who had been subjected to European colonialism were not afterwards returned to the tribal societies or imperial systems to which they had formerly belonged. Instead, leaders of the newly independent countries formed governments to take over from colonial administrators and reorganized the colonies as nation-states. As some observers have argued, they might more accurately have been referred to as 'state-nations' since the formation of the state normally preceded the establishment of national identity. During the period of colonialism, people with distinct ethnic identities were made to regard themselves as the subjects of European rulers. With the coming of constitutional independence they were encouraged to think of themselves as the citizens of newly formed but independent nation-states. The role of the nation-state in a nation-state system was never in question and this had unintended consequences for the status of people as citizens.

Prior to this, the process of European state-building based on a system of independent states had been rendered interdependent by the workings of the global economy. States were independent politically but interdependent economically. This was especially so after the first European voyages of exploration which extended European economic systems around the world and at the same time drew upon an existing pan-European economy for finance and the supply of equipment. The basis for this was trade, mainly in luxury goods, but during the twentieth century mass production and mass consumption have been spread transnationally, drawing upon the increasingly integrated resources of the global economy. In recent decades even the organization of specific manufacturing processes has become globally integrated with the further development of transnational corporations, further improvements in transport and communication, a much more developed international division of labour and new forms of support from international finance.

Global communications are of course related to these developments. Electronic technology has provided new forms of communication and the potential for their use has been hugely extended by satellite transmission systems and fibre optic cabling. Nevertheless, studies of the mass media have shown that people merely form an audience with little opportunity to respond to the images and information selected for them by specialist programme-makers, newsgatherers, or to the capacities of the technology which they use. Editors, for instance, perform the role of 'gatekeepers', letting through what they perceive to be of public interest in order to maintain the audience. Such procedures tend to remain institutionalized, and yet it is clear that the introduction of electronic technology has opened up the process somewhat. The development of microprocessors has made possible the widespread use of inexpensive personal computers which can be operated through global computer networks, particularly through the use of fibre optic cabling. Similarly, satellite broadcasting means that what is seen through the camera lens can be transmitted directly into the home on an unprecedented scale. During the Gulf War of 1990–1, for instance, images of Baghdad under fire were a regular feature on our television screens, transmitted via satellite by Western correspondents.

The relative stability of these burgeoning global systems of polity, economy and communication has been guaranteed by a world order involving the threat of military sanctions. During the period from 1945 to 1989 this was very clearly projected along the Cold War ideological split between the NATO allies of the West, led by the USA, and the Warsaw Pact, led by the USSR. A few nation-states declared themselves to be non-aligned, but the only real alternative arose during the 1970s in the shape of Arab–Islamic control of oil resources, the primary source of energy for the entire global system. Since 1989, however, the position has not been so clear. With the collapse of the Soviet Union, the USA has been left as the only 'superpower', but its economic supremacy is increasingly challenged by Japan. As a result the USA has sought economic co-operation with Canada and Mexico in the North American Free Trade Area (NAFTA) and at the same time has explored the possibilities for 'Pacific Rim' accommodation with the East Asian countries. Meanwhile the European nation-states have been struggling to find an acceptable formula for progressive socio-political, as well as economic, union. The process of globalization continues, therefore, in a world order which has lately produced three politico-economic 'cores', North America, Europe and East Asia. In the 1980s the G7 economic summits involved a group of the world's seven largest economies, measured by output, that is the USA, Japan, Germany, France, Italy, the UK and Canada. More recently, however, they have begun to be called the G3 summits, referring to the three regional cores.

Coming to terms with globalization

What I have described so far may be regarded as the structural aspects of globalization – nation-state system, global economy, global communication system and world military order. Arguably of greater significance from a sociological point of view is the nature of the society subject to these dimensions of globalization. Is it meaningful to refer to a world society? Towards the end of the twentieth century, more than ever before, people share cultural influences on a global scale and conduct significant parts of their lives in common. Moreover, people are active rather than passive in the reproduction of social institutions on the global scale. Aspects of global culture do not materialize of their own accord, they are reproduced around the world by people who thus in a sense form a global society. In order to shed some light on the reproduction of social institutions on a global scale I shall in subsequent chapters look at people as citizens (in the global polity), as producers and consumers (in the global economy), as the viewers of screens (in the global communication system) and as individuals reacting to all of this (in global social movements). All of these represent dimensions which are clearly overlapping and interconnected, but their separate discussion allows global influences upon social life to be seen more clearly. The influence of globalization penetrates the significant, the routine and the most intimate aspects of life. Globalization can be mistaken as an external influence. In fact global influences can only exist as social influences if people take them into their lives.

In classical sociology, Talcott Parsons established the principle that one of the hallmarks of modernity was the universality of social patterns. This was contrasted with the particularity of social patterns in traditional society. In the present context, globalization might be interpreted as the ultimate terrestrial expression of universality during the period of late modernity. Anthony Giddens describes this as 'disembedding', that is 'the "lifting out" of social relations from local contexts of interaction and their restructuring across indefinite spans of time-space' (1990: 21). This may be combined with his concept of the 'duality of structure' in that 'the structural properties of social systems are both medium and outcome of the practices they recursively organize' (1984: 25). Expressed another way, in drawing into their lives influences from global sources people further extend the globalization of social institutions. As such processes become further and further extended in time and space, social development in a broad sense becomes globalized.

What may be missed, however, is that when people draw global influences into their lives they do so against a background of local cultural influences. There will always be interplay between global and local influences and this has great significance for the continuing process of globalization. Roland Robertson refers to this as 'interpenetration', and he elaborates thus: 'we are, in the late twentieth century, witnesses to – and participants in – a massive, twofold process involving *the interpenetration of the universalization of particularism and the particularization of universalism . . .*' (1992: 100). On the global scale this takes the form of interpenetration between global cultural flows and local cultural patterns. The continuing development of global institutions must always be subject to this.

Many everyday practices have become heavily influenced by global cultural patterns, yet they remain part of local culture too. Eating patterns have, for instance, become subjected to the influence of effort-saving formulas and forms of globalized presentation. The much-used example of McDonald's fast-food restaurants involves a global formula both in terms of organization and of end product. The franchise for McDonald's hamburgers and their marketing has been successfully extended throughout the world. Yet clearly each McDonald's outlet is only a building and a set of equipment which is made into social reality by people who as staff and customers go about the day-to-day business of reproducing the transactions which are involved. People provide the essential human agency which is required for the reproduction of the McDonald's format. Yet they also bring to it their particular cultural experiences and preferences, and although at face value all McDonald's outlets appear to be the same, closer examination will reveal the differences. The decor and the menus are virtually identical from outlet to outlet but the actual outcome in any particular case is the result of interactions between people. In this regard the McDonald's organization is somewhat ahead of its analysts and for some time has been measuring and monitoring local differences so that they can be accommodated into the global model to maximum advantage. In Robertson's terms, as set out above, there is interpenetration between the ideal of a totally universal organizational form and the particular inclinations of customers and staff in the restaurants. Part of the reason for the success of McDonald's has been its capacity to inject flexibility into what at first appears to be the ultimate in rational organization.

The broad implication is that interpenetration between global and local cultural influences is present in all forms of social life that are subject to globalizing influences and, in the late twentieth century, that means virtually all forms of social life. This balance between the global and the local is of crucial importance in any sociological understanding of globalization. Western civilization produced the world's first truly global culture but this does not mean that Western countries continue to control it. By definition, global institutions depend for their continuing existence upon social acts of reproduction on a global scale. Furthermore, there are clear cases where non-Western cultures have been influenced by Western cultural institutions, have reproduced them amongst their own cultural patterns and have in the process added significantly to the global culture.

This can be illustrated by reference to a prime example, Japanese industrialization. Organizational patterns and techniques of industrial production were derived from the West but in their reproduction in Japan they became imbued with particular Japanese cultural influences. Subsequent analysis of Japanese industrial organization has revealed the influences of Confucian cultural patterns and of Samurai group traditions. These are held to contribute significantly to the explanation for Japan's success in manufacturing and its outperforming of the West in the global economy. Characteristic forms of horizontal organizational relationship are evident in Japanese industrial organization. The most familiar examples of this are the 'just-in-time' component supply networks known as *kanban* and also the 'quality circles' amongst workers known as *kaizen*. These have been associated with Confucian cultural influences, affecting the role of the individual in relation to authority (Kahn 1979; Wu 1985; Gayle 1986; Murakami 1986) and with the legacy of Samurai period social structure, from which is derived the essential 'groupishness' of Japanese society (Ketcham 1987; Murakami 1984, 1986). These have characterized the Japanese reproduction of industrial organization with the result that Japan has, so to speak, beaten the West at its own game of global industrial leadership.

Pursuing this example further, since Japan has had such an influence on globalized manufacturing as part of a globally integrated economy, aspects of Japanese industrial organization have been taken up by others. For example, when the American Chrysler company sought to renew its motor vehicle manufacturing after a period of extreme financial crisis, it chose to do so with significant contributions from these successful Japanese techniques. Western civilization produced the world's first truly global culture but many reactions to it, with their roots in alternative cultures, have formed part of its continuing reproduction. The result of this is that in the late twentieth century globalized culture is no longer exclusively Western. The process of reproduction and renewal in globalized social institutions is a continuing one and many, if not most, aspects of polity, economy, communication and world order have clearly become global. In fact the nature of social change is global.

This is not to say that people's participation in globalized institutions has been made more equal. The technological advances which are at the core of these developments have become more generally available globally but progress still has its 'cutting edges' in the three global regions mentioned earlier, North America, Europe and East Asia. These are the core regions within global systems in the post-Cold War period of 'late modernity'. Exploitation and glaring inequalities still exist in this world of 'triadic' politico-economic concentration, but some previous forms of analysis and critique are no longer the most appropriate. The global condition that was formerly addressed by dependency theory has become more complicated with the existence of newly industrializing countries (NICs), export-processing zones (EPZs) in less developed countries (LDCs), and a new international division of labour (NIDOL). These have brought about some changes of fortune between the 'haves' and the 'have nots' of the world. In the World Bank's calculations of per capita gross national product, for instance, Japan now has the second highest rating after Switzerland, but Singapore and Hong Kong have also entered the high income category. Additionally, South Korea and Taiwan in East Asia and Argentina and Puerto Rico in Latin America, all with very high populations, are on the threshold of that category. These brief extracts from official statistics are partial in what they convey when put into the full global context – after all the continent of Africa is hardly touched at all by industrialization – but they are indicative of change as a result of globalization.

Globalization as reflexive modernity

The main point to all of this is that political, economic and cultural institutions have been globalized. Today there is virtually no one on the planet who can participate in social life without reference to globalized institutions in some form or other. Ulrich Beck (1992, 1994) and Anthony Giddens (1990, 1991, 1994) have referred to this as 'reflexive modernity', which may be defined as a universalized form of life that touches on everyone and causes individuals to orient their actions towards it. In late modernity intensified globalization provides the individual with increased information with which to engage in social interactions. People are faced with an extending range of imagery and information involving models of citizenship, forms of production, styles of consumption, modes of communication, principles of world order and, in addition, ways of reacting to all of these. There is enhanced capacity for reflection as a result of the exposure to globalized social processes. A main consequence of this is that the individual has tended to develop increased expectations of personal fulfilment and satisfaction. This has produced various alternative or modified lifestyles. In the West the outcome might be something like 'new age travelling', but it might equally well take a more socially accepted form such as, for instance, vegetarianism. In the less developed countries it may be forms of substitute for Western lifestyles such as those provided by the 'informal economy' in the 'shanty towns'. Equally, the desire for individuality may be accommodated into the global economy in the form of flexible 'post-

Fordist' manufacturing to produce a wider choice of consumer goods or by the application of rational organizational forms to make services more widely available.

The pursuit of these individualized forms of emancipation may be termed in the broad sense 'life politics'. This distinguishes it, as a project of social development, from the emancipatory politics of early modernity which involved the attainment of citizenship rights. As Giddens puts it, 'Life-politics – concerned with human self-actualiz- ation, both on the level of the individual and collectively – emerges from the shadow which "emancipatory politics" has cast' (1991: 9). If the 'Americanization of the world' is taken to represent the culmina- tion of modernity in a materialistic sense, involving consumerism and Fordist manufacturing, then life politics embraces reflexive reactions to modernity. These include both demands for more personal choices in life, as supplied at the materialistic level by flexible post-Fordist manufacturing, and, at the same time, reactions to aspects of mod- ernity and consumerism, as illustrated by the peace movement, femi- nism, or environmentalism.

Alternatively Robertson (1992: 78–9) refers to 'globality' as 'the circumstance of extensive awareness of the world as a whole, includ- ing the species aspect of the latter'. This conflates the rise of the West, its impact on the rest of the world, and the reflexive consequences of this which he terms 'the global-human condition'. The conceptual framework for this is grounded in Ferdinand Tönnies's distinction between *Gemeinschaft* and *Gesellschaft*. A preliminary global *Gemeinschaft* would involve 'a series of relatively closed societal communities', whereas the latter-day equivalent is the 'global vil- lage'. Global *Gesellschaft* then is 'a series of open societies' and the contemporary version, 'formal, planned world organization'. The in- dication is that *Gesellschaft* is the classical sociological concept for globalization and, indeed, it was intended to signify a categorical change in the relationship between the individual and the collective. Robertson defines 'an explicitly globe-oriented perspective as one which espouses as a central aspect of its message or policy a concern with the patterning of the entire world', and, counterfactually, 'anti- globalism' as a perspective which seeks to detach from that concern.

Of relevance here is the question of the relationship between globalization and modernity. Giddens states that globalization is one of the fundamental consequences of modernity. 'Globalization – which is a process of uneven development that fragments as it co-ordinates – introduces new forms of world interdependence, in which . . . there are no others' (Giddens 1990: 174–5). Robertson disagrees and insists that 'globalization of the contemporary type was set in motion long before whatever we might mean by modernity' (Robertson 1992: 170). He also sees in globalization 'a relatively independent source of ideas about the conception of postmodernity', in relation to what he terms 'the modernity-globalization-postmodernity issue'. The resolution of this, I think, hinges on the issues that I set out earlier. That is, the reflexive aspects of the relationship between the individual and the global must be of crucial interest in contemporary sociological debate. The individual reproduces the global in day-to-day life but does so actively, not passively, and in a context of local cultural influences. This is linked with the question of what should constitute 'society' as a parameter for sociological investigation. To what extent is the experience of the individual under conditions of globalized institutions that of life in a world society? Giddens answers this as follows:

> The phase of 'reflexive modernization', marked as it is by the twin processes of globalization and the excavation of most traditional contexts of action, alters the balance between tradition and modernity. Globalization seems at first sight an 'out there' phenomenon, the development of social relations of a worldwide kind far removed from the concerns of everyday life. To the sociologist, therefore, it might appear as simply another 'field' of study, a specialism among other specialisms. The study of globalization would be the analysis of world systems, modes of interconnection which operate in the global stratosphere. So long as traditional modes of life, and especially the 'situated social community' persisted, such a view was not too far from the truth. Today, however, when the evacuation of local contexts has become so far advanced, it is quite inaccurate. Globalization is an 'in here' matter, which affects, or rather is dialectically related to, even the most intimate aspects of our lives. Indeed, what we now call intimacy, and its importance in personal relations, has been largely created by globalizing influences. (1994: 95)

The world at the end of the twentieth century is one in which it is virtually impossible for the individual human being to engage in any piece of social interaction without consciously or subconsciously relating it to social interactions on a global scale. The media of mass communication and travel bring the world to the individual and the individual to the world, on a continuous basis, so that the motivation, rationalization and reflexive monitoring of social interaction routinely include global knowledge, awareness and experience. People continually monitor the progress of their social interactions and adjust their behaviour accordingly, so much so that the process is for the most part a subconscious one. Globalization influences the reproduction of social institutions by continually presenting us with a globally derived and cumulative cultural background to inform the reflexive monitoring process in social behaviour.

The communication of global cultural information is of course centrally involved here, and increasingly electronic equipment is used for data storage, visual recording and music reproduction. The manufacture and continuing development of such equipment depends upon globally integrated production arrangements which now form a strategic part of the global economy. Additionally, tourism is a collective term for leisure travel of all kinds, the bounds of which have been extended far beyond the nation-state to the continental and the global (MacCannell 1976, 1992; Urry 1990). People also travel for work. Migrant labour in various forms, including the slave trade, was a feature of European colonialism, and since its demise 'guest workers' and more permanent immigrants have added to large-scale transfers of people on a global scale. A British Channel Four television programme provided a microcosm of this when it followed the trajectory of migrant workers from Mali, one of the poorest drought-ridden African countries. The first stop is Paris, the former colonial link, but France no longer welcomes migrant workers as it formerly did. The second possibility is New York, perhaps to work ten hours a day as a taxi driver. Then, there are the laundries and construction sites of Japan and finally the return home to 'freedom of heart, freedom of spirit' but no future.

Global movement in investment, production and labour is now commonplace. However, the economic stability created through global planning for reconstruction after the Second World War was shattered during the 1970s by a number of events. The Bretton Woods financial arrangements could not be continued in their original form and this led to greater market fluctuations. Crises in oil prices were precipitated by Arab–Israeli wars, and industrial restructuring took place on a global scale, with a new international division of labour. For a while doubts were raised about the future of capitalism, and there was speculation over what possibilities remained for self-sufficiency. The environmentalists' 'limits to growth' proposals and the *Blueprint for Survival* emerged during the early 1970s. More recently, however, faith has been restored in the global economy despite the economic recessions of the early 1980s and early 1990s. In fact, the 1980s witnessed a widespread revival for private sector economics and with this a determination to 'roll back the state'. In particular, welfare systems that had been developed during the post-war economic boom came under intense scrutiny as high interest rates forced governments to reduce substantially their public sector borrowing requirements. The decline in the provision of public services was matched to some extent by an increase in private provisions.

In 1989 the Cold War, which had held the world in thrall through the threat of mutually assured destruction, suddenly and unexpectedly came to an end. It happened more quickly than anyone, including the experts, had anticipated, and military uncertainties were added to those of polity and economy. The USA was left as the world's only superpower – but a reluctant one – and the United Nations became a renewed focus for world affairs. During the Gulf War, for instance, the USA and its military allies operated with the unequivocal backing of the Security Council for the first time in the history of the organization. The fear of nuclear war has receded somewhat but there is still the desire to find reassurance in allies, and there is now a North Atlantic Co-operation Council (NACC) which embraces both the members of the NATO and those of the now defunct Warsaw Pact. Additionally, the 1994 referendum votes of Austria, Finland and Sweden (although not Norway) in favour of joining the European Union were as much for security in an uncertain world as for economic advantage. In the face of Pacific Rim economic and perhaps political combination there is a chance that the Pacific Ocean might replace the Atlantic as the core of world affairs.

These various uncertainties – the USA no longer able, since 1970, to underwrite the global economy, the social concept of cradle-to-grave welfare apparently no longer tenable, the world order subject to a new configuration – all demonstrate two trends. First, the global inter-societal system which was created by the West is no longer under its control. Global institutions may still favour Western countries but the direction that they are taking and will take in the future is, as Robertson (1992: 62) has suggested, 'up for grabs'. Secondly, in the face of uncertainty and with traditional authority undermined, individual human beings look increasingly to personal satisfactions for fulfilment in their lives. These are the life politics of 'reflexive modernity'.

1 The European Global View

During the fourteenth to sixteenth centuries, Europeans were denied direct access to India and China by an Islamic empire that controlled the eastern Mediterranean and stretched from Spain in the west to India in the east. It was this situation that prompted Europeans to embark upon a process of maritime expansionism that was to make possible the world's first truly global culture (see table 1). The motivation for this came partly from a spiritual desire to continue the Christian crusades against Islam and partly from a much more earthly desire to engage in trade for commodities, on the supply of which Islam held a monopoly. Dom Enrique, better known as Henry the Navigator, was the Portuguese prince who is widely credited with using the ecclesiastical wealth at his disposal to set the process of maritime expansion in motion as part of continuing crusades against Islam. He was himself a medieval crusader, knighted on the battlefield and endowed with the model qualities of piety and chivalry. This contrasts starkly with Vasco da Gama, the sea captain who finally completed the route to India in 1498, nearly four decades after Henry's death. He used an Islamic pilot to guide the expedition across the Indian Ocean and went on to ensure that his surviving ships returned to Lisbon laden with commodities for which there was an established market in Europe. From neighbouring Spain, Columbus' rival voyages across the Atlantic, beginning in 1492, were also undertaken with the red cross of the crusades on the sails, but from the outset were just as clearly acquisitive. Indeed, Spanish colonialism in the Americas was threat-

Table 1 *Early stages of European global travel*

1434	Beginnings of exploration of West African coast (Eannes)
1488	Rounding of southern tip of Africa (Diaz)
1492	Atlantic Ocean crossed (Columbus)
1497	North Atlantic crossed (Cabot)
1498	India reached via the southern tip of Africa (da Gama)
1507	First recorded use of the term 'America'
1511	South China Sea entered (from the west)
1513	Central America crossed to the Pacific coast (de Balboa)
1522	First circumnavigation of the globe completed (Magellan/del Cano)

ened with abandonment in its earliest years precisely because of the paucity of the returns.

Regardless of motivation, these voyages could not have taken place without what may be referred to as global knowledge. It was not just a question of maps and navigational equipment, although these were clearly indispensable. It was also the capacity to conceive of the world as an accessible and attainable whole that could be explored and was indeed available for exploitation by those who could achieve this. In this, European attitudes contrasted with those of Islam, India or China, the other and greater civilizations during what Fernand Braudel has described as the 'long' sixteenth century of European flowering, that is 1450 to 1640. In a relatively short time, power over these other cultures was achieved through superior shipbuilding and maritime navigation coupled with superior firepower – the use of the ocean-going galleon as a floating gun platform (Cipolla 1965). The Portuguese attained their naval and commercial domination throughout the Indian Ocean and China Sea without significant territorial gain other than a chain of fortified trading enclaves. By contrast the Spanish in the Americas took all before them and in the process completed the destruction of three civilizations: the Aztec and the Maya in Central America and the Inca of the Andes.

A significantly distinctive aspect of Europe was its constitution, not, since the fall of Rome, as a unified empire, but instead as a collection of separate sovereign states and smaller political entities (Hall 1985: 133–40). Others soon followed in the wake of the Portuguese and the Spanish. The absence of any overriding power is illustrated by the failure of these two to maintain their early monopoly of colonialism, despite the fact that they had in principle divided the entire world outside of Europe between themselves. The Treaty of Tordesillas, which was based upon a notional longitudinal line 1,500 miles to the west of Cape Verde, endowed everything west of the line to Spain and east of it to Portugal. It received the official assent of the Borgia pope, Alexander VI, in 1494 and it is a notable piece of European arrogance. As Barnet Litvinoff (1991: 137) puts it, 'It was as if no other power, Christian or otherwise, could contemplate building a ship that might sail an ocean.' It could not be enforced for long however – not because there were any non-European contenders but precisely because there was competition between the European states. Litvinoff (p. 139) describes it thus: 'The Christian nations were divided and bent upon each other's humiliation, even destruction, whereas Islam militant embraced a monolith ruled by a despot from its summit at Constantinople.' European merchant adventurers, operating out of home bases that formed parts of an existing interdependent pan-European market system, had buying-power sufficient to ensure success, often without needing to use military force against anyone. The now notorious Atlantic slave trade was so economically attractive at the time that all the European states were drawn in, and they could count on the complicity of West African tribal chiefs against other tribes, such were the potential advantages of trade with Europeans.

The Europeans added what can best be interpreted as organizational ability to a series of technological advances derived indirectly from the other great civilizations. As a result, the compass from China, the astrolabe from Islam and the lateen sail from India, together with gunpowder, also from China, were developed to ensure that Europe, backed up with military force, drew ahead and stayed ahead of the other cultures in navigation and commerce. The instruments of navigation were combined with improvements in shipbuilding while the more precise metal-casting of cannon barrels was combined with the organization of gunnery schools. The use of the printing press was combined with the widespread publication of literature, including treatises on mathematics that could be used in bookkeeping as much as in navigation or gunnery. None of these things were developed to anything like the same degree in Islam, India or China. Later on, the Industrial Revolution was to provide the manufacturing capacity for Europeans completely to supersede alternative manufacturing industries in other parts of the world.

Navigation and shipbuilding did not just involve manufacturing and transport expertise, however; they also provided the vital thread of global knowledge and communication. They made possible the creation of a long-distance communication system that soon became global. As the Portuguese pressed eastwards across the Indian Ocean and into the China Sea, the Spanish pressed westwards beyond the Americas and across the Pacific, until the two met up. These beginnings are clearly a significant factor in the extension of European culture as the world's first truly global culture. Oceanic travel and communication became routine for Europeans. At first only a tiny proportion of the population was involved, but later many more were drawn in through emigration to 'new worlds'. For centuries this development was extremely gradual, given the limitations of sailing-ships in the face of adverse weather conditions, but later the introduction of steamships, trans-oceanic cables, telegraphy, broadcasting and aircraft led to today's world of fast travel and instantaneous communication.

Throughout this long historical process the ability of Europeans to reproduce their institutions around the world by means of superior communications is clearly apparent. These institutions include not only religion and trade but also the politico-military mechanisms developed in Europe as part of an expanding state administration. This allowed for the centralized administration of territory, the resultant concentration of revenue collection, and the enhanced maintenance of the whole arrangement through the provision of standing armies with a monopoly of the means of violence. These developments represent the extension of European colonialism. Ultimately, however, processes of cultural spread through global communication have also involved the projection of certain aspects of the West's developing societal model which stand in contradiction to colonialism itself. These were the enshrinement of the Enlightenment principles of equality before the law, political participation and the utilization of talent from the whole population through the provision of opportunity and the recognition of achievement. These principles of modernity were characteristically Western, and yet they worked against European colonialism. Ultimately, the education of colonial subjects as 'native administrators' produced a class of people capable of using European institutions against Europeans. But modern Europe's characteristic ideals of liberty and equality are in themselves merely principles and their fulfilment or the lack of it has been just as much a part of Western culture. The global systems created by Europeans have taken Western institutions to the whole world but they have nowhere provided the means to ensure the distribution of its benefits in anything like equitable proportions.

As with scientific advances, these socio-political advances had in some respects been pre-empted by Europe's cultural adversaries. A case in point is the principle of qualification through performance in written examinations which had existed in Chinese empires for centuries with the aim of improving imperial service through appointment by achievement rather than ascription. In other civilizations, however, such institutions did not contribute to modernization as they did in the West.

The global and the everyday

Probably the single most important factor in the globalization process is that images derived from social institutions that have become globalized enter into our day-to-day reproduction of society. During Braudel's 'long' sixteenth century certain privileged or gifted individuals in Europe began to develop a perspective on the world that interpreted it as an accessible whole. Nowadays such a world view is commonplace and enters into all of our social activities. Indeed it is difficult to enter into any piece of social interaction without consciously or subconsciously relating it to global patterns. Commonplace illustrations of this are easily called to mind. For instance, we go to the supermarket conscious of a range of produce that is global in origin, mindful not only of globally projected images of its worth and benefits but also of the possible effect of our purchases on such things as Arctic whaling or the Amazon rain forest. To take a very different example, part of the Brazilian underclass plays football on the beach with images of the World Cup, its implications and its ramifications, not just vaguely but rather clearly in mind.

Roland Robertson (1992: 170) argues that 'globalization of the contemporary type was set in motion long before whatever we might mean by modernity'. But elsewhere (p. 53) he explains that 'the concept of globalization *per se* is most clearly applicable to a particular series of relatively recent developments concerning *the concrete structuration of the world as a whole.*' In Anthony Giddens's (1990) terms this might be referred to as a 'discontinuity of modernity', in the sense that there is a very significant distinction to be made between the creation of globalizing institutions historically and their routine reproduction as a reflexive process in the fully globalized world of late modernity. Furthermore, European maritime expansionism set in motion social processes that created global systems of communications, polity, economy, and so on, but in the late twentieth century these institutionalized forms have been developed in such a way that they are no longer exclusively under the control of Europeans. As early as 1909 Mahatma Gandhi was able to observe that 'there is no such thing as Western or European civilization, but there is a modern civilization'. His statement was clearly part of an anticolonial ideology designed to diminish the image of the West, but it was none the less an acute observation, particularly for the time. Once created, global systems are by their very nature open to global participants. Furthermore, since their routine reproduction depends upon the contributions of participants on a global scale, the form of global institutions continues to change. This is a point which Robertson himself regards as essential for the adequate conceptualizing of globalization.

> rather than emphasizing the crystallized structure of the world system, a voluntaristic theory remains sensitive to empirical developments, and thus stresses the processes of globalization and the continuing contentiousness of global order. One of my basic points is that varying responses to globalization influence that very process, so that its direction and outcome, and hence the shape of the global field itself are still very much 'up for grabs'. (Robertson 1992: 62)

In the earlier quotation Robertson uses the word 'structuration' deliberately, although he professes to have problems with the concept as propagated by Giddens. He asserts that in order to be useful the term 'has to contribute to the understanding of how the global "system" has been and continues to be *made*'. This would seem to pose no problems since the single most important principle of structuration theory is that social institutions exist in concrete terms only in the passing moment of time as patterns of social interaction reproduced by human beings. The extension of social institutions through time and space, to global proportions, must always be the result of their social reproduction. Moreover, the process is not a passive one but is intrinsically active. It is conditional for the continued existence of any social institution that it must actively be reproduced, and in the act of reproduction there exists the capacity for transformation. As Robertson puts it, the varying responses to globalization influence the process, as in his reference to the term 'glocalize', which is derived from Japanese marketing practice and means roughly 'global localization', or the global 'in conjunction' with the local (p. 173). Broadly speaking, Robertson's argument involves a principle derived from Immanuel Wallerstein's work (1984: 166–7):

> the attempt to preserve direct attention *both* to particularity and difference *and* to universality and homogeneity. It rests largely on the thesis that we are, in the late twentieth century, witnesses to – and participants in – a massive, twofold process involving *the interpenetration of the universalization of particularism and the particularization of universalism.* . . . (Robertson 1992: 100)

The most important principle of globalization to be addressed here is, I think, the combination of Giddens's principles for structuration in the reproduction of society and Robertson's concept of the 'interpenetration' of the universal and the particular. This will form a thread throughout. In this chapter, however, I want to pursue the creation of a European world view as the foundation for globalization, before going on in later chapters to examine the dimensions of contemporary globalization.

The European world view

In his *History of the World* John Roberts writes of the 'European mind' in the creation of a European civilization which by 1500 was clearly recognizable (1992: 427). He is referring to a collective consciousness embracing a sense of identity, of history, of progression and of spatial awareness extending to the limits of a definable world. Its origins lay in Christianity which was at the time synonymous with the European identity and which, through its translations into Latin and its copying of Latin texts, was the carrier of classical civilization through the so-called Dark Ages to the Renaissance. The first European universities at Bologna (1158), Paris (1179) and Oxford (1219) are an important outcome of this, with their formative faculties of law, medicine, theology and philosophy. The process of development involved inputs from other civilizations and particularly from Islam, Christianity's rival as a 'world religion' and Europe's neighbouring civilization to the east. Mathematics, astronomy (originally coupled with astrology) and medicine came to Europe in important part from Islam, although, in the case of Ptolemy's work, it could be argued that Europe was merely retrieving from Islam what was originally its own Greek legacy. Other influences, beyond Islam, came from India and China with which Europe had no direct contact until after the oceanic voyages of Christopher Columbus and Vasco da Gama. Amongst these inputs was the printing press. This had had little impact in China but the crucial difference in Europe was the mode of its adoption. It was used to make an existing body of literature more widely available, and this proved to be emancipatory in its broadening of access to knowledge. The use of the press also coincided with the pioneering oceanic voyages. Gutenberg's press was first set up in 1455 during the period when Portuguese mariners were extending their sea-borne explorations down the west coast of Africa, preparatory to entering the Indian Ocean, and less than four decades before Columbus' first crossing of the Atlantic. Europeans were extending their mental horizons through communication with the printed word as well as through ocean-going voyages. The foundations were being laid for global systems in communication, politics, economics and the military.

In his more specific work, *The Triumph of the West*, Roberts stresses the difference between European and other civilizations and notes that, strangely, this has often been regarded as unremarkable (1985: 176). Europeans were able to look out upon the rest of the world in ways that other civilizations could not or would not match. In one graphic example of the conceptual differences, Roberts points out that the West could produce, amongst its dramatic literature of the seventeenth century, Dryden's insights into court life and the succession of a Mogul emperor in his play *The Indian Emperor*. This was at a time when it can safely be assumed that no Indian ever wrote about comparable European court politics (p. 176). For Roberts the broadness of the European approach to the rest of the world confirms that the motivation was not just greed which, after all, other civilizations had too. In fact economistic explanations for the rise of the West simply will not suffice on their own, despite the huge amount of social science writing devoted to them. The driving force was a much broader form of aggrandizement based on a sense of superiority and destiny derived from a uniquely European notion of history and progress. Thus Roberts emphasizes (p. 177) that, for instance, Europeans became better cartographers, although others had the skills first, and that they dramatically improved upon existing metal-casting skills so as to build more effective weapons. Advances such as these were part of a broad cultural sweep which facilitated and at the same time was itself facilitated by the acquisition of technologies from the east. There was also the purchasing of luxuries, commodities to which Europeans had hitherto been denied direct access, together with the more practical supplies of grain and timber from southern Russia. The process was a cumulative one (p. 179) in which the crusading spirit, exemplified by the desire to unite with the mythical Prester John in a final sweep against the flanks of Islam, was developed into a much greater project involving nothing less than the global spread of European culture. The first slaves brought back to Portugal from the west coast of Africa were deemed to be 'moors', or 'blackamoors', and therefore prisoners of war. In the long term the outcome was hugely influential involving nothing less than the creation of a transatlantic core to a global culture, the widespread exploitation of non-Europeans and, subsequently, the inevitable reaction against this. In 1481 the pope prohibited the sale of firearms to Africans (p. 194) but their use in capturing slaves for the Atlantic trade ensured that it was not effective for long in preventing the spread of European military institutions. The unintended consequences (p. 184) of Henry the Navigator's initial efforts to facilitate oceanic communication are enormous.

Running through all of these developments is the crucial definition of the world as it existed in the minds of Europeans and the way in which this contrasted with Europe's rival cultures. A consistent theme of this book will be the relationship between the global and the individual. In the manner described here, the European world view became augmented by ambition, practical achievement and the setting down of permanent records in the form of maps and other documents. Ptolemy's *Geographia* was important in both European and Arabic scholarship, but it was Europeans who translated the concept of a finite and accessible world into pragmatic actions. Consequently it is European usages that have become global usages. The earliest European world maps have Jerusalem at the centre and are a combination of geographical knowledge and biblical conventions. But as the word 'Europe' replaced 'Christendom' in normal usage, and Byzantium was removed as a rival Christian civilization, world maps came to have Europe at the centre with the other continents on the margins. The conception of having sufficient politico-military power to divide up the world, implicit in the Hispano-Portuguese Treaty of Tordesillas of 1494, was made unworkable, not by any other civilization but by the increasing activities of other European states. The familiar layout of a world map encompasses 'Eurocentrism' as the normal order of things and, almost universally, other cultures have fallen in with this. For example, the Chinese imperial view of itself as the 'middle kingdom' between heaven and the rest of the world disappeared as it came under the thrall of, first, Western modernity in Sun Yat-sen's republican revolution of 1912, and then a form of counter-modernity in Mao Zedong's communist revolution of 1948. Long before then, the idea of a New World – Amerigo Vespucci's *mundus novus* – was of space for Europeans and an extension of European culture. In the nineteenth century, the zero meridian was set, by an international convention of Western states, to pass through Greenwich and so fix topographical and navigational co-ordinates for the rest of the planet. It is said that this was prompted largely by timetabling difficulties with the Canadian Pacific Railway, one of the earliest efforts to reduce a vast 'new' continent to the dimensions of domestic travel and communication. In more recent times the distinctions between a First, Second and Third World have been used to divide the West notionally from other cultures and these distinctions, too, were drawn up by Europeans according to their own definitions (Worsley 1984: 307).

The broad cultural outcome has been something which Gerrit W. Gong has defined in terms of 'the standard of civilization in international society', a set of requirements clear enough by the beginning of the twentieth century to form 'an explicit legal principle and an integral part of the doctrines of international law' (1984: 14). In the classical tradition of the West, this has much to do with the Greek notion of the 'civilized' and the 'barbarian'. The rediscovery of antiquity by humanists and the voyages of discovery by navigators were turning-points, at more or less the same time, in Europe's cultural and intellectual history. From then until the twentieth century significant aspects of the rise of the West were an overweening confidence, a sense of achievement and superiority and the belief that there was little to learn from the rest of the world. Indeed this is part of the Western distinction between tradition and modernity which gave rise to much of the sociological tradition. Durkheim's definitions of social solidarity and the division of labour and those of Weber on forms of rationality and patterns of authority are derived from this, albeit they involve critique. Western culture was seen as modern and civilized whilst the rest was traditional and irrational. Moreover, during the nineteenth century the enthusiasm for scientific and technological advances determined that there was relatively little problem with this overriding distinction. In practice of course the rise of the West depended upon much that was learned from elsewhere, as I have outlined above. During the twentieth century, as people in the West have become less confident of their advantages and as doubts have grown about the superiority of Western culture, a different distinction has been created. The concept of post-modernity has been conceived to describe a condition contrasted with modernity and associated with principles directly opposed to those on which the rise of the West was so confidently based. Nevertheless, world history has been overwhelmingly European history because of the very fact that it was Europeans who first acquired a pragmatic and workable world view. Once the world had been viewed in this way and propagated as such, it became increasingly difficult for other cultures to come out of the shadow of the West. When they have subsequently achieved this, it has been in the context of an existing Westernized, globalized world and institutional forms employed against the West have themselves been Western and global in nature. By the same token the globalized world, created initially by European maritime expansionism, has come to be no longer exclusively under the control of the West. Its institutions have become available for others to exploit, as in the prime case of Japanese industrialism.

The Renaissance and the Enlightenment

William McNeill (1985: 42) describes the rise of the West in terms of stimuli to social change, from 50 BC onwards, provided by a 'Eurasian ecumene' of contact between the civilizations of the Mediterranean, India and China. The outcome was a 'global ecumene' consolidated by the end of the eighteenth century. As Jan Aart Scholte (1993: 10) points out, this gradual approach contrasts with Robertson's special emphasis on a 'crucial take-off period of globalization' during the late nineteenth and early twentieth centuries or Giddens's onset of truly globalized society during the late twentieth century. I think that there is room for both the long-term and the more recently pitched approaches. The notion of a 'global ecumene' encapsulates rather well the idea of a spread of European influence as part of which Western social institutions were implanted throughout the world. Then, during the eighteenth and nineteenth centuries, the artefacts of Western civilization came to be produced on the increased scale which industrialization made possible. Thereafter came the export of whole packages of industrialized Western culture, such as the railway systems which made transcontinental transport and communication into regular and routinized everyday events. From this is derived Robertson's insistence upon the late nineteenth century as the take-off of globalization. Equally it is the Western innovations of the twentieth century, like the broadcasting of sounds and images or the marketing of products with universal appeal, that constitute Giddens's requirements for a truly globalized world in which the individual cannot avoid coming into contact with the global. I would argue that the rise of the West through maritime expansion and the subsequent industrialization of its productive capacity can be inter-preted as the creative process for social institutions that by the late twentieth century are truly global in form. During this latter period, perhaps after 1960, it has become apparent that global institutions are, as Robertson (1992: 62) has suggested, quite clearly 'up for grabs'. That is, the global systems set up by the West are no longer completely under its control and there have emerged counter-influ-ences. Major examples of these are the rise of industrialism in Japan and subsequently throughout East Asia, or the resurgence of Islam in renewed forms, utilizing Western institutions like the nation-state and taking advantage of the global reliance upon energy derived from oil.

Litvinoff (1991) argues for the importance of 1492, the year in which the possibility of the Ottoman Turks emerging from their eastern Mediterranean base was effectively eliminated by Columbus' Atlantic crossing. Thus was assured European domination of ocean routes, significant until the mid-twentieth century. He links this to the sweep of the Renaissance northwards, through cultural influences, such as the works of Michelangelo or Leonardo da Vinci, and political influences, such as those derived from Machiavelli and the struggles between the Medicis and Borgias. There were economic influences too as in the case of Venetian *partes*, which were invest- ment shares in mercantile voyages; or the institutions of exchange developed at the Rialto bridge; or the principles of *partita doppia* (double-entry bookkeeping) set out by Luca Pacioli in Florence. These were crucial developments in the social institutions which Europe was to implant around the world. Litvinoff (1991: 48) de- scribes how 'printing had the effect of reducing the importance of Latin and stimulating national cultures', which of course were to be the essential political forms of a globally powerful Europe. He also describes the reflexive influence of globalizing institutions on na- tional cultures, and the difficulties facing the Portuguese throughout their long chain of overseas possessions:

> Those extensive lines of communication, the cost of fortifications and the burdens posed by the constant threat to the Portuguese, both on the high seas and on land, could overwhelm the tiny motherland. He [King Manuel] therefore encouraged actual Portuguese settlement, as had already begun in Brazil, in India first and then in Africa, with Catholic marriage to local women. This would strengthen the individual personal stake in the empire. Commerce was ostensibly a government monopoly – a fifth of all profit to the crown – but huge sums dropped into the wrong pockets. Try as the viceroy might to stem the haemorrhage by tightening regulation of the markets, theft persisted all along the 12,000 mile line; that and flagrant corruption, with the result that Lisbon's prosperity enriched the international merchants swarming round the honey pot whilst the Portuguese as a whole remained poor. Except for the older African trade in slaves, gold and ivory, insufficient revenue reached the king's treasury to cover the ever-spiraling expense of polic- ing the enormous endeavour, not to mention the loss of life entailed. By the time of his death in 1521 King Manuel, far from being the wealthiest monarch, was deep in debt to foreign bankers. (Litvinoff 1991: 251)

As for the Portuguese, Alan K. Smith (1991: 76–8) refers to a lack of certainty about what they were doing – but at the same time he looks upon the end result as outstandingly successful. What he means is that efforts to make a broad success of their colonial ventures tended to result in the singular pursuit of economic wealth, whether for the crown or for other interests. The Spanish, on the other hand, who at first had much less experience of maritime exploration, soon embarked upon a supremely confident programme of prodigious empire-building. The plunder of two civilizations, Cortés against the Aztec and Pissarro against the Inca, were carried out by small groups against superior numbers. This contrasted with the initial doubts about Columbus' lack of gains and it led to widespread exploitation extending through the Americas. In other respects, however, the Spanish experience was much more similar to that of the Portuguese. Charles V, a Habsburg king of Spain, derived vast wealth from silver mines in the New World. But since he was also Holy Roman Emperor it tended to be disbursed throughout his empire, which covered parts of central Europe and Italy as well as Spain. He attempted to develop his imperial interests by borrowing from bankers in reasonable anticipation of further silver imports, but this tended to benefit commercial infrastructures, especially in the core mercantile centres of the time at Antwerp and Genoa (Braudel 1984: 150–1). His successor to the Spanish crown was Philippe II; he was not hampered by additional responsibilities for the Holy Roman Empire, but the strategic problems did not go away. There were opportunities enough in the colonies, but at home both Spain and Portugal lacked the kind of infrastructure needed to supply fully the material needs for socio-economic development. Consequently this task fell to a variety of artisans, notaries, financiers and merchants across Europe, with consequences for the broader social fabric. In some cases their activities were extended into ventures that stretched westwards across the Atlantic and eastwards into the Indian Ocean and the China Sea. There is a domestic side to colonialism. It is not just the milieu of adventurers and administrators, and the exchanges which were created led to extensive cultural development. Before 1492 Europe had no potatoes, tomatoes, green beans, peppers – or chocolate. This list includes commodities which, combined with the noodles that Marco Polo had earlier introduced from China, form the basis for Italian cuisine as we know it today. By the same token, until that date there could be no 'traditional' Mexican beef *tacos* or cheese *quesadillas* because beef, lamb and dairy products were unknown hitherto on that side of the Atlantic.

In broader perspective, Robertson (1992: 58) refers to a 'germinal phase' – 'lasting in Europe from the early fifteenth to the mid-eighteenth century' – as part of what he refers to as 'the temporal-historical path to the present circumstances of a very high degree of global density and complexity'. He draws attention to the growth of national communities and the accompanying decline of a 'medieval trans-nationalism' in Europe, counterpoised with an extension of the influence of the Catholic Church. A consequence of this was an expansion of the role of scribe and scholar, with ramifications for the study of humanity and its place in time and space – for example 'the spread of the Gregorian calendar' and the 'heliocentric theory of the world and beginning of modern geography' (p. 58). Medieval transnationalism in Europe was broken up by increasingly powerful state structures – the beginnings of a state system – which were able to nurture extending global economic connections – the global economy. The 'germinal phase' is, in Robertson's terms, succeeded by other temporal phases, including the crucial 'take-off phase' during which 'globalizing tendencies' give way to a 'single, inexorable form' (p. 59). This is linked to his key concept of interpenetration between universalisms and particularisms which he attributes in part to Arjun Appadurai's 'twin Enlightenment ideas of the triumphantly universal and the resiliently particular' (Appadurai 1990: 308).

Anthony Smith's comparable linking of the 'national ideal' with 'a certain vision of the world' (1979: 2) is also taken up by Robertson to argue that '*the idea* of nationalism (or particularism) develops *only* in tandem with internationalism' (1992: 103). Elsewhere (p. 56), he has cited James Der Derian's (1989: 3) observed coincidence of Jeremy Bentham's advocated need for the word 'international' with the declaration of the 'rights of man' in the French Revolution of 1789. There would appear to be much evidence, from the early Portuguese–Spanish rivalry onwards, for the conjunction of nationalism and a state system with an international perspective. Der Derian lists 'the development of elective powers in medieval Christendom (such as Venice and the Swiss Confederation); the rejection of monarchic rule and adoption of republicanism by the Dutch in the sixteenth century; the contractual doctrine of legitimacy that came out of Britain's Glorious Revolution in the seventeenth century; and in the United States, the institutionalization of popular politics by the Continental Congress of 1776' (p. 3). This may sound suspiciously like a tautology because the very creation of states must imply internationalism, but the point is that political entities become outward-looking precisely through their awareness of other political entities. The Treaty of Tordesillas was signed only two years after Columbus' first voyage, and this is arguably the first significantly global agreement by European states. A treaty was seen as necessary for dealing with rival claims to territory but it is no doubt significant that, in the process of negotiation, King John II of Portugal was knowledgeable enough geographically to have the line moved further west than at first envisaged, so acquiring for himself the considerable prize of Brazil (Litvinoff 1991: 137). By contrast with this early European example of international relations, the other civilizations have tended to be politically and economically monolithic, dismissive of rival claims, and as a result their perspectives have been inward-looking. In these cases, the empire in a sense *was* the world and anything outside of it unworthy of attention. In the Roman empire there had been the classical distinction between the civilized and the barbarian, derived from the Greeks. The Chinese regarded any outsiders in a similar fashion and wanted nothing to do with them. The fourteenth-century oceanic explorations of the Chinese admiral, Cheng Huo, preceded those of the Portuguese and Spanish by a century, but they were brought to an abrupt end by an imperial edict under which they were regarded as undesirable.

Narrowing the emphasis to specific links between states, Scholte suggests that 'international interdependence has . . . been sealed over the centuries through money' (1993: 59). He refers to the symbolic nature of money as something exchangeable internationally with a significant degree of trust. An example of this is the circulation of reliable currencies in Europe, as in the case of the Venetian *ducato* which was recognized throughout the Mediterranean area during the Renaissance – or the Hispano-Mexican silver dollar in the post-Columbian Atlantic trade. The latter is especially interesting because it became an accepted form of currency even in China during the period when the Chinese, in their imperial isolation, would accept only silver in trade with Europeans. Much later, after the Second World War, there was international agreement in the form of the UN-sponsored Bretton Woods financial arrangements under which currencies were linked to the US dollar and the dollar to gold. In this broad context, Scholte (p. 69) refers to the concept of the 'international regime', taken from the study of international relations. There are antecedents to this in the European imposition of the Julian calendar with its Gregorian reform and the Greenwich meridian mentioned earlier. There is also the establishment of norms for warfare which in fact crop up in both European and Indian civilization – but it is the Geneva Convention, first held in 1864, that is recognized today. Other international regimes of modernity include such arrangements as the International Telegraph Union of 1865 or the Universal Postal Union of 1875, both of which are now under the

United Nations' aegis. They were established for regulatory purposes in the interests of the modern nation-state system and they signified that the world was becoming globalized.

A rather obvious but no less significant symbol of globalization is the application of European names to places as part of an assertion of superior geographical knowledge and techniques. This has caused people to recognize parts of the natural environment, such as rivers or mountains, in a manner that is globally convenient but which clearly carries implications for the onlooker's relationship with the culture that imposed the nomenclature. For example, the name 'Victoria Falls' clearly conveys British imperialism and the existence of a powerful monarchy and yet it has survived decolonization in modern-day Zambia and Zimbabwe. There is a broader set of examples containing European imagery in the names of the continents. Europe is consistently the powerful centre of the world, often visually symbolized by the bull. Asia is seen as rich but barbaric, reflecting past relationships – at the same time desirable and awful to the European. America is named after Amerigo Vespucci of Florence, the transatlantic adventurer to whom is credited the origin of the term New World. Africa is taken from the name of the Roman province which took the place of Carthage in North Africa after its destruction. Australasia is straightforwardly the southern continent, but of course in European definition. Long before any of these names were applied there was the overland route between the Mediterranean and China which has existed from earliest antiquity. It was not travelled by Europeans until the thirteenth century when the Polo family of Venice made their journeys to China. Much more recently, during the 1870s, the name 'Silk Road' was applied by the German explorer, Ferdinand von Richthofen (Thubron 1989: 121). Now it is as though the European name has always existed and it is used by people far removed spatially from Europe but brought under its influence through contact with the usages of global communication.

The standard of civilization

Gong's (1984) reference to a notion of 'the standard of civilization in international society' has already been mentioned in connection with the desire of other cultures to fall in line with European expectations. It expresses the sense in which Eurocentric expectations are seen as necessary or desirable by non-Europeans and, as such, serve as a legitimation device for cultural imperialism in its various forms. Robertson (1992: 121) points to the very different examples of Sun Yat-sen's republican China in 1912 and post-revolutionary Russia in 1918 (quoting Zerubavel 1981). Despite sweeping change to the social order it was felt necessary in each of these cases to respect conventions of Western society in order to enjoy the benefits of an international order. Robertson uses this to argue that Elias's (1982) account of the civilizing process takes insufficient account of the ways in which the process operates as a regulative mechanism, particularly in state formation in relation to the global nation-state system. Robertson sees the 'standard of civilization' as having a globalizing effect on international relations during the first half of the twentieth century and reaching its zenith during the 1920s. One could possibly go further to state that both revolutions cited here were to a significant extent Eurocentric in their conception. Sun Yat-sen was the son of a Christian farmer, educated in exile, first in Honolulu where his elder brother lived and then in British missionary circles in Hong Kong. As with so many nationalist leaders who have risen up to throw off outdated regimes, including those of European colonialism itself, it could be expected that the Western institutions in which Sun Yat-sen had become encultured would play an important part in the achievement of his objectives. The nation-state which was created in the name of republican China was to all intents and purposes a Western institution in constitutional terms and its processes involved many aspects of Western culture such as status, procedures, and forms of dress. The formation of states in relation to the modern nation-state system is an important dimension of the overall globalization process; chapter 3 is dedicated to the further examination of this.

Contrasting with the issue of entry to Western-dominated global systems is the question of non-entry. An example is Japan's chosen isolation from Western influence during the Tokugawa period, which Robertson (1992: 85) nevertheless regards as 'a globally oriented gesture'. That is, it was, by implication, an acknowledgement of global power and a dangerously pervasive social order, which the Japanese Shogunate consciously chose to avoid. When, however, Japan's institutions were eventually brought into the arena of global systems it was, Robertson insists, through a combination of Western inducement and voluntaristic processes. In fact, Japan became not only a participant but also a pacesetter. Following the outstanding success of post-Second World War Japanese industrialism and indeed as part of the process, other East Asian countries have, as Robertson puts it, 'learned how to learn' in terms of modernization. This contrasts starkly with the failure of Latin American countries to learn how to learn and their consequent inability to influence significantly global systems, despite their continental association with the USA.

It is the reasons for this distinction between success and failure that throw light on the question not only of participation in global systems but also of influence and significance in the continuing globalization process. With his continued interest in the religious aspects of such developments, Robertson (p. 89) stresses the importance of secular aspects of the development of Japan. The influence of Confucian philosophy is apparent throughout more than 2,000 years of East Asian history, but the incursions of Buddhism and to a lesser extent Christianity into Japanese society were relatively unimportant for the modernization process. Instead there is the 'discovery' (p. 94) of an indigenous religion, Shinto. This became a state religion and it has consistently contained elements of the Confucian requirement for loyalty. Observers such as Michio Morishima (1982) have distinguished the emphasis on *loyalty* which is apparent in Japanese Confucianism from that on *beneficence* in Chinese Confucianism. During the Meiji restoration, state Shinto was used in the manner of a code of ethics to ensure loyalty to the emperor and, reflecting modernization, to accommodate Western views on the differentiation of church and state (p. 89). This lasted until Second World War defeat in 1945, after which state Shinto was abolished by the occupying Americans, who insisted on their own value of religious freedom in its place. The removal of Shinto does not, however, imply the removal of the underlying Confucian philosophy or code of ethics in contemporary Japanese culture. Many writers (e.g. Kahn 1979) have pointed to the importance of Confucian principles in the Japanese rise to industrial power. What is seen as a 'post-Confucian' stress on loyalty is taken as being as significant for the new industrial structure as an earlier form was for the old imperial regime. For present purposes this is strong evidence for the argument that the reproduction of global institutions involves the particularization of the universal as well as the universalization of the particular. A significant part of Japan's rise to global power has been based on a revitalized form of industrialism in which that nation's reproduction of Western global institutions came to involve what is now a rather obvious capacity to influence the broader outcome. What is now recognized as post-Fordist manufacturing contains a range of approaches to socialized production involving not just the labour process but the entirety of commodity acquisition, transformation and distribution. The global systems created by the West were, in the terms mentioned earlier, 'up for grabs', and Japan, with a broader East Asian infrastructure in support, has influenced global communications, the global economy and to a lesser extent the nation-state system. Japan became a member of G7, the group of the seven most economically powerful states in the world, and this gave it political as well as economic power. At the same time its non-participation in the military aspects of world order since the Second World War has freed it to concentrate on other aspects of international relations, such as the activities of its renowned Ministry of International Trade and Industry (MITI). This has undoubtedly enhanced its socio-economic progress.

The process of globalization is often taken to be an imposed process – the rise of the West and the imposition of its institutions around the world. In fact, to repeat a constant theme, social institutions do not reproduce themselves but have to be reproduced by human beings. However forceful some aspects of European colonialism undoubtedly were, there had to be voluntaristic processes involving the reproduction of its social institutions in order for it to become a continuing process of globalization. In this sense the globalization process admits of pluralistic influences. Western institutions are reproduced in the widest variety of physical and cultural situations and it is precisely this pluralism that produces the particularization of the universal which accompanies the universalization of the particular. Western civilization *is* the world's first truly global culture and as such it has provided parameters for subsequent societal development. In a sense, under the conditions of late modernity, society is world society. That is, the individual everywhere has to come to terms with social institutions that have become global institutions. But the pervasiveness of Western institutions does not amount to absolute uniformity or anything approaching it. There is a relationship between globality and pluralism through which pluralism contributes to cultural advance. The West, despite a tendency to deny the fact, transformed its own culture into a global culture precisely through contact with a plurality of other cultures. But the other side of the relationship is that globalization relies upon the pluralistic reproduction of globally recognized institutions in order for the process to continue. Friedrich Tenbruck (1990) argues that the very notion of societal progress is a global one, that, in idealized form, the world is viewed as a 'secular ecumene' – as for instance characterized by UNESCO's vision of a just world through education. But to this must be added that once created the global system is, as I emphasize here, 'up for grabs', and progress may not always be as initially and ideally envisaged. What was once taken as inevitable progress through enlightenment, the modernization project, has proved to be far from uni-directional and this has given rise amongst other things to notions of post-modernity.

All of this is an extremely generalized treatment of globalization, however, and in ensuing chapters the subject will be divided up into dimensions of communication, states, economy, the military and social movements. First, however, I will address the creation of global institutions in terms of what may be described as the twentieth-century project. This is the extension of mass participation society, through its dimensions of mass production, mass communication and mass consumption. It is the phase often referred to as 'the Americanization of the world' – desirable in terms of lifestyle but eminently criticizable on the grounds of exploitation. It is also the historical phase in which major doubts arise as to the validity of the rise of the West and its globalization processes.

2 Mass Society and the American Dream

Arguably the most significant difference between tradition and modernity lies in the access that people have to the benefits of 'civilization'. In medieval Europe for instance, as in all traditional societies, that which constituted civilization existed only in the courts of the nobility and the higher clergy, and the houses of wealthy merchants. For the great mass of the population life on the land was basic, deprived and little different from that of tribal society. The domestic and the ordinary was neglected and downtrodden in favour of the culture of an elite who had more in common with their contemporaries elsewhere than with the peasantry on their own land. In stark contrast to this, modernity has provided the capacity for whole populations to participate in an emancipated culture with the benefits of enlightened citizenship, mass production for mass consumption and of course mass communication. Moreover, the parameters of this type of society have become globalized as part of its continuing development. Mass society is essentially linked with globalization. Richard Rosecrance has observed that the distinction between the traditional and the modern 'represents a reordering in the priority of international and domestic realms. In the medieval period, the world, or transnational, environment was primary, the domestic secondary' (1986: 77). To some extent the creation and development of more powerful sovereign states inhibited the transnational environment that had existed previously. But this effect was counteracted by the opening up of well-endowed courts to the patronage of arts and scholarship which encouraged further international exchange of ideas. Roland Robertson (1992: 54) writes of 'the de-unification of medieval Europe' but qualifies this on the basis that 'the rise of the territorial state also promoted imperialism and thus conceptions of the world as a whole'.

The important point here is that in the transition from traditional society to modernity there has been a fundamental change of emphasis which is particularly apparent in late modernity. The early cultural development of Western civilization involved international exchange, but it impinged on only a small proportion of the population, the elite. By contrast, during the twentieth century 'mass society' has, as its name suggests, involved the great mass of the population in its advances. Furthermore, its benefits (and its disadvantages) have been mass produced for mass consumption on a global scale. This is clearly connected with the development of American society during the twentieth century. The much-used phrase, the American dream, refers, perhaps idealistically, to greatly improved material standards of living for masses of people hitherto denied such opportunities (see table 2). Arguably, this is an extension of the principle of participation in society as enshrined in the American constitution. It is, in a sense, an economic equivalent of the political 'rights of man and the citizen' on which the United States of America was founded. Manifestly, it does not represent the extension of equal benefits to all, any more than the Declaration of Independence meant in practice that 'all men are equal', let alone women. But in the development of mass participation society there is a clear principle that hugely increased numbers of people gain access to material benefits and to knowledge through mass communications. Forms of democratization, both political and economic, contrast with the privileged social processes of the old order. Furthermore, as people have drawn these things into their lives the form of Western social institutions and therefore of global social institutions has continued to develop.

To a great extent the USA achieved its power and influence in the world from a position of relative isolation. This may sound a contradiction in terms and it is certainly an irony. Yet it was through internal expansion on an unprecedented scale that greatness was achieved. There is the physical dimension to this in the extension of the 'frontier' westwards until the eastern and western seaboards were linked – first by wagon trail, then by railway and telegraph, and more recently by the most extensive and sophisticated travel and com-

Table 2 *Some twentieth-century American developments of global significance*

1890	First moving picture show staged in New York
1900	Andrew Carnegie publishes *The Gospel of Wealth*
	Human speech transmitted by radio waves
1903	First powered flight
	Ford Motor Company founded
1907	Immigration restricted by law
	First daily comic strip
1908	Harvard Business School founded
	General Motors Corporation formed
	Ford Model T produced – beginnings of mass production
1909	Commercial production of bakelite – beginnings of plastics industry
1910	The weekend becomes popular in the USA
1912	Woolworth Company founded
1913	Ford begin full-scale assembly-line production
1915	Ford produces millionth car and develops a farm tractor
	First transcontinental telephone call
1918	Airmail services introduced
	Daylight saving time introduced
1919	First non-stop transatlantic flight
	First radio broadcasting station opened
1924	Ford produces 10-millionth car
	2.5 million radios in use in USA
1927	15-millionth Model T Ford produced
1928	First scheduled television broadcasts
	First colour motion pictures

Source: Bernard Grun, 1991: *The Timetables of History*. 3rd edn, New York: Simon and Schuster/Touchstone Press. Repr. with permission.

munication network in the world. In the course of this process the 'pioneers' created the space for mass immigration and established, despite a bitter civil war, a federation of states, each with its own identity but strongly imbued with the supra-state principles of American nationality. Within this huge spatial opportunity, the founding ethos of mass participation and equal opportunity, which was an explicit breakaway from European tradition and privilege, was established. Furthermore it was extended from the constitutional spheres of law and politics, through the economic principle of 'free enterprise', into concrete practices of production and communication that could deliver to everyone – mass consumption. The enabling dimensions to this were Fordist manufacturing, unprecedented marketing techniques and the American dream of consumer culture. But alongside these were the constraining forces of continued inequalities in wealth, virulent racism, and organized crime that was every bit as innovative as legitimate enterprise. The importance attached to principles of freedom, representative democracy and equal opportunity has given rise in many cases to less desirable forms of enterprise. For instance, in the recent past an Act of Congress has allowed federally recognized Indian tribes the freedom to operate gambling whenever that form of gambling already exists in the white-dominated parts of the state where they reside. In Connecticut a minority Indian tribe has been able to open a casino because such an activity already existed as a fundraising activity for the Roman Catholic Church. In a rather bizarre global link, the Indian operation was set up with investment from a Malaysian family already heavily committed to the gambling industry internationally, and especially in East Asia where of course gambling is a passion. These are some of the unintended consequences of policies of freedom and equality of opportunity.

Even some of the negative aspects to the characteristically American process of democratization and free enterprise are, however, indicative of the Americanization of the world. The great crash on Wall Street in 1929 precipitated the Great Depression of the 1930s, which had repercussions not only in Western agriculture and manufacturing, but also in diverse activities around the world. Banking in central and eastern Europe was affected, with the notable failure of the Austrian Kreditanstalt bank. The progress of Soviet industrialization was noticeably interrupted, although it was passed off at the time as 'growing pains' and contrasted with the 'collapse of capitalism in the West'. Throughout most of Asia there was an impact on the level of domestic rice prices. In Africa the export value of the products of the European colonies declined as the world market prices of cash crops plummeted (Davidson 1994: 51–2). This brought home the extent to which American finance was linked to the global economy and it gave clear indications that this was increasingly interdependent.

Yet the Wall Street crash has to be seen as another manifestation of mass participation – of 'the American way'. More people than ever before had the chance to speculate in capitalist investment and, in this sense, it represented a form of social emancipation. But the process of expansion became so over-extended that it collapsed. In more recent times, ways have been found for the financial markets to extend participation and therefore capital accumulation much further, while at the same time guarding against the dangers of the complete system failure of 1929. On so-called 'black Monday', 19 October 1987, twice as much value was lost from Western stock markets as in 1929, yet global finance was able to absorb the losses much more effectively.

If the principles of mass society depend upon legal and political mechanisms, the material aspects depend upon the trinity of mass production, mass communication and mass consumption. In the USA the assembly-line techniques of Fordist mass production first made mass consumption possible, but mass communication is equally important as the medium of information about participation in the process. In communication, the electric telegraph was developed to follow the railway tracks and supersede the Pony Express in the transmission of messages across the vast distances of the North American continent. This preceded the telephone and made possible the monumental step, now taken for granted, of eliminating the need for a human messenger and greatly increasing the speed of transmission. However, given the scale of late twentieth-century communication, it is not surprising that this seems only a modest advance when compared with broadcasting, satellite transmission and the use of fibre optic technology in globalized mass communications. In fact, it was various combinations of the telephone, radio, cinema, popular music, and ultimately television that provided the essential lubrication of mass communication to the dual 'generators' of twentieth-century Americanization, mass production and mass consumption. The economic formula for Henry Ford's success in manufacturing was quite simply that if money could be made from supplying relatively few well-off people with a product, much more could be made from putting that product within the means of all people. The principle on which this is based is an instrumental one, yet it is undeniable that in the process participation and access to consumption is achieved by greater numbers of people. Despite all the brutalities and iniquities of mass production, Ford pioneered the mass consumption of manufactured products. In so doing he established the principle of paying the workers sufficiently for them to become consumers of their own collective products – thus extending the market.

Put together, the constitutional principles on which the USA was founded and the revolutionary changes in production and consumption which took place there during the early twentieth century represent the extension socially of a much broader range of institutions. These social institutions reached far beyond the USA and this has given rise to the concept of globalization. Right from the start Ford was manufacturing for a world market and his first car, the Model T, was envisaged as a 'world car'. The broad social change involved is not unlike what Émile Durkheim was referring to with his distinction between the mechanical and the organic in social solidarity and the division of labour. The difference is between a small-scale society, enclosed within its own schedule of activities and relationships, and one on a much larger scale in which much greater numbers of people share common knowledge and experience, engaging in a different order of social relationships on that basis. The pioneering constitutional arrangements developed in the USA and the economic opportunities of a new society attracted large numbers of immigrants from Europe during the onset of mass production and consumption. The Statue of Liberty remains an icon of what, in principle at least, was offered to the immigrants, and it is significant that the statue came from France, the other example of constitutional history hugely transformed by a late eighteenth-century revolution. The USA was a former European colony in the New World, transformed into an independent receptacle for people seeking to avoid either Europe's old iniquities or the new ones created by the various political changes which swept through the continent during the nineteenth century. The United States government became an advocate of constitutional change elsewhere: above all it called for an end to European colonialism. Indeed, American participation in the Second World War can be seen in retrospect to be at least partially tied to an insistence on progress towards ending colonialism after the war. The commitment to self-government in the Atlantic Charter of 1942 was testament to that.

In materialist terms, the Fordist manufacturing formula was swiftly transported beyond the USA as a complete production package. A plant to produce the Model T was opened in England, at Trafford Park in Manchester in 1911, at the same time that substantial production levels were being developed in the USA. Immediately Ford's plans extended along the major lines of global cultural flow as they existed at the time, and these were still in the form of European colonialism. In the United Kingdom, Ford plants were set up to supply the home market and the British colonies overseas, while similar arrangements were made in other European countries. In Latin America, however, with the decline of Spain and Portugal and the constitutional independence of their colonies, Ford's US plants set out to supply virtually the whole of the Americas. These developments coincide more or less with Robertson's (1992: 59) 'take-off' and 'struggle-for-hegemony' phases in the progress to globalization, or what he refers to as 'a very high degree of global density and complexity'. By the 1960s, however, the end of European colonialism was more or less complete and Robertson's 'uncertainty' phase begins, with the process of globalization following new dimensions. These new dimensions are principally the achievement of fully globalized media for:

- *politics* – with a mature nation-state system symbolized by the workings of the United Nations, dedicated to an international 'declaration of human rights'.
- *economy* – the Bretton Woods financial arrangements as a foundation of international 'modernization', ostensibly for the benefit of less developed countries but involving Western industrialism and culminating in the creation of globalized mass production and consumption – chiefly by Western transnational corporations but leading to a New International Division of Labour involving newly industrializing countries (Fröbel et al. 1980).
- *communication* – with the beginnings of the 'electronic revolution' in information storage and globalized communications.
- *the military* – with the Cold War confrontation and its two opposing alliances (NATO and the Warsaw Pact) influencing virtually all instances of military conflict.

These global systems were opened to freer participation after the 1960s by the combined effects of two things. The first was the end of European colonialism and the second the decline of US domination both in politico-military terms, with defeat in the Vietnam War, and in economic terms, with the end of dollar–gold convertibility in 1970. Each of these changes contributed to a situation in which globalized institutions created by the expansion of Western civilization come to be 'up for grabs' in conditions no longer controlled by Western nation-states. Although the USA remains the most powerful nation-state, it has found it impossible to maintain absolute power in politico-military or economic terms. Japan, meanwhile, has transformed itself from a recently modernized nation-state into the world's most successful manufacturing country. Furthermore, its investments in plant have been extended not only throughout East Asia and elsewhere, but, significantly, into the industrial heartlands of Europe and North America.

Rationalization

Both the liberal-democratic form of government and the Fordist system of mass production represent examples of the formal rationality which Max Weber observed as characteristic of Western society in its modernization process. Weber noted that the principle was capable of application to all forms of social organization. Impersonal bureaucracy is created to deal with large-scale activity on a routine basis and at the same time to detach administration from personal preference and sectional interest by creating formal rules of procedure. Bureaucracy was in fact Weber's paradigm case of formal rationality. 'Legal–rational bureaucracy' provides an appropriate formula for organization under the conditions of modernity. The practice does not always conform to the formula, as countless studies have shown, but its persistence alone guarantees its importance in the analysis of Western society and its global influence. The secret ballot and representative democracy, on the one hand, and bureaucratic office involving appointment through achievement on the other, are cornerstones of Western culture applied to government and its attendant administration. There is no direct economic equivalent to this because for several centuries economy has in principle been separated from polity in Western society. In the process polity has moved entirely into the public domain, especially through the development of the state, while, by contrast, economy has been maintained as the sector of private enterprise. This has remained so despite various ideological attempts to extend the state's influence in recognition of industry's dependence on socialized labour.

However, this is not to deny that formal rationality and the practice of bureaucracy are applied to production in the privately owned economic sector. Frederick Winslow Taylor's principles of 'scientific management' are especially significant here chiefly because notice was taken of them in the USA at the turn of the century, precisely the place and the time of the revolutionary changes in manufacturing which made mass production possible. Indeed Taylor's own studies were in the US steel industry where advances in metal-cutting provided some of the basic techniques necessary for the mass production of consumer goods. Scientific management gave rise to 'time and motion studies', a detailed analysis of work processes in order to eliminate any wasteful effort, and 'cost and works accountancy', the incorporation of the former into financial calculation. This is quite clearly the case of Western formal rationality applied to work. It involves the separation of the management of work from its execution and the relinquishment of control and responsibility on the part of the worker. Ford added to Taylor's principles by completely redesigning the workplace to accommodate the rationalization of assembly-line manufacturing. In the British Industrial Revolution, Arkwright's 'water-frame' and Crompton's 'mule' rendered textile manufacturing impossible other than in factories, whereas previously it could take place in all kinds of workshops and even in the home. Fordist manufacturing required not only factory premises but ultimately buildings constructed around the layout of the conveyor-belt production line. The Ford chronicler, Booton Herndon, describes the initial attempts as follows:

> When they first attempted to assemble an entire car by the assembly line method, they put a frame on skids and pulled it from one end of the building to the other with a rope. A group of men walked along with it, grabbing parts from pre-placed piles as they went along. The next refinement was to station different men, or teams, by the equipment, and drag the chassis past them. In this crude second-generation method, the frame had to stop while the men performed their assigned operations. To allow for the fact that some operations took longer than others, the interval between each production was increased or decreased. As the process was refined, the number of man hours per car was cut from 15.5 to 1.5. (Herndon 1970: 90–1)

The refinement of the process, as it is described here, amounts to a socio-technical system in which the technology of the motor car is broken down and rendered into a form that provides for a new technology of manufacturing. In order to ensure maximum productivity scientific management required the removal from the workers of responsibility for their own actions in the labour process, but the assembly line took this several stages further, with the division of labour extended and work reduced to its lowest common denominator. Such work involves skills which are mechanical, taking only the minimum of time to learn, carried out at a uniform pace set by the machinery. There is no pleasure or satisfaction for the worker and work becomes purely instrumental for pay, far removed from the creativity of craft production. The rationale for the arrangement is that the goods are produced in large quantities, standardized at a certain quality and emerge at a price which most consumers can afford. This really is the combination of mass production and mass consumption. At this point we may seem to have moved away from the subject of globalization, yet the two elements of scale and standardization are quite clear. The individual, either in the production process or in the act of consumption, is confronted with experience that is common to greater and greater numbers of people over a wider and wider area. Nevertheless, there is an important distinction to be made in contemporary examples of organizational rationalization. Henry Ford's ethos of standardization, 'you can have it in any colour that you like so long as it is black', no longer applies and indeed is no longer acceptable. Today's rationalization is flexible, geared towards notions of access to choice and the individualism of the consumer, even if these are somewhat contrived and partially illusory.

George Ritzer (1993) picks up the theme of contemporary rationalization as applied to the provision of products and services. His definition of 'McDonaldization' is 'the process by which the principles of the fast-food restaurant are coming to dominate more and more sectors of American society as well as the rest of the world' (p. 1). His argument is that the principle is now applied not only to 'the restaurant business, but also education, work, travel, leisure-time activities, dieting, politics, the family, and virtually every other sector of society' (p. 1). Clearly there is evidence for this and it cannot have escaped anyone's notice that, for instance, repeated complaints about food at railway and bus stations have resulted in a plethora of fast-food outlets, or that what used to be called the Labour Exchange in Britain is now called the Job Centre which, even from its public sector base, presents similar if toned down aspirations to those of a fast-food restaurant in terms of the reception and treatment of clients. Ritzer is appreciative of the benefits of the principle. The placing of goods and services at a certain guaranteed quality within the reach of people who would otherwise be denied them is a form of democratization; as Ritzer puts it, 'The fast-food restaurant has expanded the alternatives available to consumers. For example, more people now have ready access to Italian, Mexican, Chinese and Cajun foods. A McDonaldized society is, in this sense, more egalitarian' (p. 14). But he is also concerned, as was Max Weber before him, about the dehumanizing effects of rationalization applied to so many aspects of society. For Ritzer, the principle of 'McDonaldization' is the culmination of bureaucracy, scientific management and the assembly-line method, albeit in flexible post-Fordist form. Its application to fast-food restaurants is only a prime example of a principle applied to many aspects of society in late modernity. For the present work the significance of this is, of course, the globalization of the model. The appearance of McDonald's outlets in virtually every part of the world has been successful even in areas where the culture includes a strong culinary tradition. This is only indicative of a broader trend involving the widespread adoption of the Western formal rationality and its effective application to many forms of social organization. Concern over the banality of fast food is, for instance, repeated in the case of fears that the 'Disneyfication' of children's entertainment stultifies children's imagination with predigested imagery. Ritzer describes many examples of rationalized forms of organization which were developed on a large scale in the USA but which have been spread globally. The list can be expanded as follows:

> overhead trolley systems in slaughterhouses (the source of Henry Ford's inspiration for the assembly line)
> assembly-line production of 'consumer durable' products, e.g. television sets, washing machines, etc.
> systematized food-processing
> system-building in housing and other building applications
> supermarkets, shopping malls and home-shopping networks
> fast-food restaurants in a variety of specializations
> automatic drink and food dispensers
> franchising of successful marketing formulae
> standardized hotel chains (Go and Pine 1995)
> self-service filling stations and mini-markets
> motor-car lubrication, tyre and exhaust centres

drive-in forms in a number of service industries
banking with cash machines and telephone banking
postal services with 'zip' or postal codes
formats for 'blockbuster' entertainment with ancillary marketing
microwave ovens in home cooking
multi-service medical centres in place of the doctor's surgery
package tours to global destinations
dietary and medical systems for cosmetic purposes
recreation/holidays in vehicle form – caravans, campers, etc.
multiple-choice, machine-graded assessment in education
'modular' courses and semesters in universities
broadcasting and electronic media in religious worship
'digested' media – e.g. *Readers' Digest, Time, Newsweek*, etc.
the marketing of sport – and sport as a marketing opportunity

It is arguable that access to higher standards of living is just as much a process of democratization as political emancipation and that similar inequalities of power and wealth attend the outcomes in either case. The projection of the model of a consumer society throughout the world, by means of the very system of mass communications that forms a part of it, has brought about the kind of reflexive transformations in social mores that are at the heart of the globalization debate. Individuals see the model and attempt to reproduce it in their own lives, but this is never a passive process. Institutions cannot reproduce themselves but are subject to human agency in their reproduction. Therefore Western institutions, which are undoubtedly pervasive around the world, are nevertheless not passively received but are subject to all kinds of interpretation in the process of their globalized reproduction. As I emphasize throughout this book, there is an interpenetration between the global and the local by which people draw global developments into their everyday lives. These reflexive transformations have created new norms in people's expectations of living standards and consumption patterns everywhere. As a consequence of this, new markets for goods and services have been created, notwithstanding the glaring inequalities in access, delivery and fulfilment, within as well as between nation-states.

In the subsequent chapters there will be many examples of these forms but I want now to turn to the significance of the USA during the twentieth century. I approach this both in terms of the USA's own collective estimation of itself and the influence of American institutions elsewhere, even against open hostility.

The convergence thesis

It was as early as 1901 that Wilfrid Scawen Blunt published his treatise, *The Americanization of the World*, and the theme is one that has often been taken up since then, especially in the face of the erosion of local cultures by cosmopolitan influences. One way in which American social science picked up on this process is expressed in terms of the 'convergence thesis', the idea that all societies are converging in form on one model. The model is characterized by industrialism, and of course resembles the US model, with high levels of mass production and mass consumption. The classic exposition of this is *Industrialism and Industrial Man* by a group of American labour economists (Kerr et al. 1960), who believed 'that the future [would] see the complete triumph of industrialism'. They wrote in terms of a 'logic of industrialism' and, as with much of the writing on modernization, the starting-point was the British Industrial Revolution. Put simply, this produced the world's first industrial society, but when British progress slowed down or was overtaken, American enterprise went on to transform industrial society into mass production society. The prime concern of these authors was with labour relations and the future of these in 'the age of total industrialization'. They saw this as a central issue for any theory of culture and society in an age of advanced industrialism. However, a postscript was added to the book in 1973 and the convergence thesis was made more explicit to express the belief that the logic of industrialism is capable of transcending all cultural and ideological differences between societies. The historical background to this was, first, the great ideological divide of the time between US capitalism and Soviet state socialism, coupled with the implicit belief that the rationality of US society must triumph over the irrationality of the Soviet system. Secondly, the 1960s was the decade when European colonialism was brought to an end and industrialization was seen as the way forward for the 'developing countries'. The envisaged global dimensions of industrialized production and consumption are presented in this postscript as clearer than at first expected:

In expanding their modern sector enclaves, for example, the developing countries have generally had less difficulty in overcoming cultural barriers than we anticipated. Constraints such as the family structure, class and race, or religious and ethical values have seldom impeded rapid development in the modern sectors. Nearly all of the less developed countries have modern office buildings, hotels, factories, airports, and highways in the urban areas. Coca-Cola, Bata shoes, Hilton Hotels, TV, and grocery supermarkets are almost as ubiquitous in Abidjan, Lagos, Addis Ababa, or Bogota as they are in Copenhagen, Berlin or Tokyo. The new culture of the cities acts like a magnet drawing ever larger numbers of migrants from the rural areas who quickly conform to a new culture of urban life. (Kerr et al. 1973: 282)

The attractions of the modern are taken to be universal and their form is clearly American. In this work and commonly throughout American social science (Ross 1991) the USA is regarded as occupying a special position in history.

Both modernization theory and the special position of the USA have been heavily criticized since the convergence thesis was first propagated and yet the pervasiveness of the institutions referred to by Kerr et al. and subsequently by Ritzer can hardly be doubted. This is a cue for drawing attention back to one of the central points of globalization, the conjunction of universalistic and particularistic trends in the globalization process. Institutions which become globalized can only develop in that way through their active reproduction in all parts of the world. This act of reproduction is the crucial sequence and it is at this point that the universal becomes conjoined with the particular. It is here where the notion of Americanization breaks down because the institutions are reproduced in other cultures and the outcome can never be as uniform as the term would suggest. Globalization is therefore a better term. When the process of reproduction of social institutions is adequately taken into account what tends to be perceived as outright cultural imperialism instead takes more the form of a reflexive process. In the course of their extension on a global scale, social institutions are rendered open or, as described by Robertson, 'up for grabs'. Upon reflection, a globalized institution must by definition be one open to global influences. It must be discernible across cultural differences and, incidentally, across the constitutional borders of nation-states which are themselves global reproductions of a Western institution. Above all, once created, a system of globalized institutions becomes subject to a global variety of counter-influences.

It is necessary at this point to affirm that the use of the term 'open' in this context is not meant to imply equality of access. The phrase 'up for grabs' is more appropriate because, as it implies, globalization involves the participation of ever larger numbers of people. In this sense it is emancipatory. But such participation can take place only in conjunction with social institutions of a political and economic nature, and these have also been subjected to Western influence on a global scale. The origins of globalization are Western and Western political and economic institutions are reproduced as part of the process. There are inequalities inherent in these, and more inequalities are introduced in the course of their reproduction in other cultures. The establishment of the Western nation-state and liberal democracy in constitutionally independent post-colonial countries has provided a distressingly large number of examples of this. At a more modest level of social organization, returning to Ritzer's example, despite the precise reproduction of the trade marks, despite the precise formula for the hamburger, one McDonald's fast-food restaurant is not the exact replica of another. Each example is the production of the people, workers and customers, who come together to make it a working institution. At the same time, legal titles, management procedures, pay structures, pricing formulas and other regulatory mechanisms are reproduced as part of the social process and these result in it incorporating inequalities similar to Western inequalities.

In retrospect, it appears logical that descriptions of the decline of US power in the world, as addressed by the Reagan presidency, should have emerged during the late 1970s and early 1980s, the same time as descriptions also emerged of a new international division of labour, global production lines, newly industrializing countries and globalizing tendencies in general (Fröbel et al. 1980). They are all terms used to describe the restructuring of social relations to such an extent that, arguably, the definition of society for social science study should be moved from the nation-state, the previously normative parameter, to the world or world society. There is perhaps an exemplar for this in the case of international finance and currency regulation. In 1944, the Bretton Woods financial arrangements were created to ensure that international financial relations could be conducted on a secure basis and that the kinds of problems which arose after the First World War might be avoided. The anchor for the system was the US dollar and its routine convertibility to gold. All other currencies then had a fixed exchange rate with the dollar and thus the system virtually guaranteed their value. Adjustments were made, when necessary, in the form of revaluations or devaluations, with the agreement of the World Bank and the International Monetary Fund. However, by the late 1960s the USA had accumulated an increasingly adverse balance of payments situation, worsened by such disparate factors as the escalation of the Vietnam War and the increase of imports from burgeoning East Asian industrialization. As a result a US government commission of inquiry, the Pearson Commission, recommended that dollar–gold convertibility be brought to an end. This recommendation came into effect in 1970 and since then the world's currencies have been subject to money market fluctuations on a day-to-day basis, with occasional devaluations and revaluations on top of that. In short, the USA could no longer sustain its regulation of the world's currency patterns and these became subject to a global system in which they were, to use Robertson's phrase again, 'up for grabs'. Moreover, this occurred during a period when US military power was put in doubt by the débâcle of the Vietnam War, when a US president resigned to avoid impeachment; and when the Arab–Islamic nations were bringing their economic power to bear against the West through the OPEC cartel and the manipulation of oil prices. All of these are examples of global systems of polity and economy, created by the West or to Western patterns, but developing beyond its control.

In politics, the nation-state system had been transformed, largely because of the establishment of the United Nations in 1945 and the end of European colonialism during the 1960s. It had developed to become a means whereby many different manifestations of ethnicity or nationality might assume a constitutional identity through adopting the Western nation-state model within a global system of international relations. The nation-state system was itself overlaid by the global military order in which the two Cold War superpowers, the USA and the USSR, competed vigorously for relative diplomatic influence and strategic advantage. They did this through their respective military alliances, NATO and the Warsaw Pact, while overall the nuclear threat of mutual assured destruction held them in permanent stalemate. Meanwhile, throughout the 1970s and 1980s, global production lines and a new international division of labour were developed through a system of global economy freed from Western domination and no longer restricted to a financial system controlled by the USA. In this context, Japan and the newly industrializing countries of East Asia, plus some others in Latin America, were taking an increasing share of global manufacturing.

Nevertheless, as Robertson counsels, the apparent decline in the power of the USA should not be exaggerated. With the removal of the Soviet Union it remains easily the strongest military power. At the same time it has had to reverse its previous anti-UN stance in order to try and 'fuse the future of the United Nations with American self-interest'. As Robertson (1992: 118–19) puts it, 'the USA now has the problem of legitimizing its position as the guarantor of "world peace", of denying to every additional nation the right to overwhelming warlike nuclear and "post-nuclear" power'. This is done against a background of 'the expanding international presence of Japan and Germany'. Thus the USA has encountered growing difficulties with its global politico-military role while those examples of rationalization in organizational forms, developed and applied to day-to-day life as part of the American dream, are now reproduced by others as post-Fordist rationalization. That is, not only are they reproduced by others but in many cases they are improved upon and even introduced into the USA in improved form. This has, of course, contributed to the USA's increased economic difficulties as it comes to terms with the existence of global institutions over which it no longer has the influence that it once did.

3 The Citizen in the Nation-State System

In the perspective of world history the relationship between the individual and society can be seen in a variety of political and constitutional forms. The broad variations might, however, be abbreviated into three types for purposes of analysis, as follows: the individual as member of a tribe; as the subject of some form of ruler; and as the citizen of a nation-state. There are of course many variations within these three and such a simple typology has the disadvantage that it does violence to the finer detail of historical narrative. Nevertheless, in sociological terms, it is useful to distinguish between the position of the individual in:

- *tribal society* – where the individual's existence is typically as part of an extended kinship system
- *'civilization'* – where the individual's existence is typically as part of a 'class-divided society' – the ruling function or state is contained in some kind of urban administrative centre amidst a rural hinterland, and within its walls an elite made up of nobility, higher priesthood, wealthy merchants and their attendants lives a 'civilized' urban existence separate from the rural peasantry on the land
- *Western civilization as modernity* – where the individual's existence is typically as citizen in a nation-state consisting of a designated national population within fixed territorial borders – the social division between town and countryside has been broken

down and the entire population engages in the processes of mass society:

mass participation in politics through representative government

mass participation in economics through mass production and mass consumption

mass participation culturally through mass communication

However, the study of modern Western societies tends to have been undertaken within the parameters of the nation-state, while towards the end of the twentieth century this typology might be extended further in recognition of the globalization of social institutions. Processes of globalization have routinely involved the individual in a range of social institutions that are transnational in their effects. Therefore, while the nation-state is undoubtedly still significant, it should no longer be the only, nor even perhaps the foremost, parameter for society as it is studied by social scientists. Rather there needs to be a concept of world society that encompasses the study of global institutions and the relationship between the individual and the global. This implies the addition of a fourth type to the list:

- *global society in late modernity* – in which the individual's existence increasingly has reference to global institutions:

    in the political sphere through the nation-state system, international relations and the United Nations

    in the economic sphere through global production/consumption and the international division of labour

    in the cultural sphere through global communications

    in the military sphere through world order, regional blocs and nuclear weapons

    and also in relation to global movements in peace, feminism, environmentalism, etc.

Clearly, there is a sense in which the universal adoption of the Western model of the nation-state has represented a rational and bureaucratic standardization of the state form, compared with its comparatively random traditional forms in pre-modern civilizations. This is not to say that all nation-states are the same. Clearly they are not, but the remarkable thing about the contemporary nation-state system is the universality of the model for the nation-state and the consistency in principle of its constituent elements. Combinations of representative government, bureaucratic administration, independent judiciary and forces of coercion with a monopoly of the legitimate means of violence are standard. The existence of the model as the norm is evident through such things as the long-standing protocols of diplomacy in international relations and the more recent existence of the United Nations Organization as a global forum for all nation-states (see table 3). International lawyers have referred to the existing form of relationship between sovereign states as the Westphalian model, after the Peace of Westphalia of 1648. In sociological terms the development of these relationships between states might be regarded as a prime example of Max Weber's formal rationality. There is considerable standardization both in the structure of the individual nation-state and in its capacity to form the basis for a system of nation-states. Within a nation-state legal–rational bureaucracy exists in the form of centralized administration and techniques for surveillance of the population. In other types of society administration tends to be local, random and much more subject to the influence and caprice of significant individuals. Post-Enlightenment society has involved the production, in T. H. Marshall's terms, of:

- liberal-democratic forms of political citizenship with the state as authority
- equality of civil citizenship with the state as law-enforcer
- enlightened social citizenship with the state as carer

All are present in the nation-state model, albeit subject to imperfections and irregularities in practice. The most significant aspect is undoubtedly the universality of the model.

It might be argued therefore that the modern era of mass society has represented for individual human beings a process of standardization in their relationship with the state – and furthermore that each nation-state has formed part of a global nation-state system. Marshall's terms, as set out above, now reflect the expectations of the individual under liberal democracy. As expectations they have become virtually universal and this is confirmed by the expressions of dissatisfaction, outrage and protest that are elicited when the terms are abused or ignored. However, the globalized society of late modernity has come to involve so many different transnational pro-

Table 3 *United Nations membership*[a]

1945	Argentina, Australia, Belgium, Byelorussian Soviet Socialist Republic,[b] Bolivia, Brazil, Canada, Chile, Republic of China (Taiwan), Colombia, Costa Rica, Cuba, Czechoslovakia, Denmark, Dominican Republic, Ecuador, Egypt, El Salvador, Ethiopia, France, Greece, Guatemala, Haiti, Honduras, India, Iran, Iraq, Lebanon, Liberia, Luxembourg, Mexico, Netherlands, New Zealand, Nicaragua, Norway, Panama, Paraguay, Peru, Philippines, Poland, Saudi Arabia, South Africa, Syria, Turkey, Ukrainian Soviet Socialist Republic,[b] USSR, USA, UK, Uruguay, Venezuela, Yugoslavia
1946	Afghanistan, Iceland, Sweden, Thailand
1947	Pakistan, Yemen
1948	Burma
1949	Israel
1950	Indonesia
1955	Albania, Austria, Bulgaria, Cambodia, Sri Lanka, Finland, Hungary, Ireland, Italy, Jordan, Laos, Libya, Nepal, Portugal, Romania, Spain
1956	Japan, Morocco, Sudan, Tunisia
1957	Ghana, Malaysia
1958	Guinea
1960	Benin, Burkina Faso, Cameroon, Central African Republic, Chad, Congo, Ivory Coast, Cyprus, Gabon, Madagascar, Mali, Niger, Nigeria, Senegal, Somalia, Togo, Zaire
1961	Mauritania, Mongolia, Sierra Leone, Tanzania
1962	Algeria, Burundi, Jamaica, Rwanda, Trinidad and Tobago, Uganda
1963	Kenya, Kuwait
1964	Malawi, Malta, Zambia
1965	Gambia, Maldives, Singapore
1966	Barbados, Botswana, Guyana, Lesotho
1968	Equatorial Guinea, Mauritius, Swaziland
1970	Fiji
1971	Bahrain, Bhutan, Oman, People's Republic of China (membership of Republic of China/Taiwan revoked), Qatar, United Arab Emirates
1973	Bahamas, East Germany, West Germany
1974	Bangla Desh, Grenada, Guinea Bissau
1975	Cape Verde, Comoros, Mozambique, Papua New Guinea, São Tomé and Principe, Surinam
1976	Angola, Seychelles, Western Samoa
1977	Djibouti, Vietnam

Table 3 *Continued*

1978	Dominica, Solomon Islands
1979	St Lucia
1980	St Vincent and the Grenadines, Zimbabwe
1981	Antigua and Barbuda, Belize, Vanuatu
1983	St Christopher and Nevis
1984	Brunei
1990	Namibia, Yemen; also a united Germany replaced East and West Germany
1991	Estonia, Latvia, Lithuania, Marshall Islands, Micronesia, North Korea, South Korea, USSR's membership replaced by Russian Federation
1992	Armenia, Azerbaijan, Kazakhstan, Kirgizia, Moldova, San Marino, Tadzhikistan, Turkmenistan, Uzbekistan

[a] Dates are dates of joining; current names in English are used.
[b] In 1945 the USSR negotiated membership for two of its constituent Soviet Socialist Republics to counteract its minority status.

cesses that the focus for the relationship between the individual and authority must be seen as changing. The nation-state system remains important, of that there can be no doubt, and so does the ubiquity of the nation-state model, but additionally there has been increasing restructuring in international relationships. Amongst other things, the end of the Cold War has contrasted the success of the USA as a vast federation of states with the failure of the Soviet Union's alternative model. There is also the continuing effort of European nation-states to extend their co-operation from economic community to social, political and economic union, and the attempts, much less understood in the West, to explore the potential for co-operation between East Asian nation-states. These attempts revolve around the economic success of Japan, the expectation of further politico-economic change in China and the potential for a common 'post-Confucian' culture across that whole area. However, before going on to discuss the effects of such changes on contemporary relationships between citizen and nation-state, I propose to examine some often-neglected aspects of the Western model of the nation-state as they have affected the individual. Inasmuch as the nation-state is a global model and its origins are Western, these are important for understanding global projections of citizenship.

The Western model of the state

Much has been written about the creation of the nation-state model as a thoroughgoing Western project. I should like to direct attention at this point to the work of Francisco Ramirez and John Boli (1987) on the political construction of mass schooling as part of the Western state project. I do this because I think that it provides a good example of what has already been described as the imposition of a 'standard of civilization' – the pervasive influence of Western patterns on state-building and development throughout the world. Moreover, it does so in a way that emphasizes the relationship between the individual and the state in terms of ideals and expectations in modernity – the concept of the 'achievement society' and individual self-improvement. I want to examine this before going on to explore how such a relationship might be changed by processes of globalization.

Education and more particularly state-sponsored mass education is, in modernity, the primary source of formal socialization facing the individual as citizen of a nation-state. Ramirez and Boli's approach embraces both its enabling and constraining aspects. Their view is that nation-state authority and educational opportunity are corner-stones of a global model for national development. This, they argue, is affirmed by the virtually universal acceptance of educational goals as an intrinsic part of the ideology of the nation-state and the creation of constitutional forms for their attainment. They follow Edward Reisner's (1922) and Yehudi Cohen's (1970, 1979) line of argument that a state project such as mass schooling could only occur in Western civilization's distinctive political format of competing separate sovereign states. Ramirez and Boli (1987: 3) acknowledge the conditions which produced cultural, political and economic change in Europe, that is 'the Reformation and Counter-Reformation, the construction of the national state and interstate system, and the triumph of the exchange economy'. Their chief observation is that these broad transformations 'produced a model of the national society that emphasized both the primacy of the socializable individual [Berger, Berger and Kellner 1973] and the ultimate authority and national responsibility of the state [Grew 1984]'. Their main point is developed from an earlier work (Ramirez and Boli 1982) which argued that the adoption of mass education represents 'a highly institutionalized model of national development throughout the world'. Included in this is a sense of enablement, as the individual is given access to 'knowledge' and the opportunity of becoming 'educated'. But enablement is combined with constraint upon the individual to identify with and participate in the state as a national project. As these writers put it:

> Our view is that European states became engaged in authorizing, funding, and managing mass schooling as part of an endeavour to construct a unified national polity [cf. Ringer 1977; Bendix 1964]. Within such a polity, individuals were expected to find their primary identification with the nation, and it was presumed that state power would be enhanced by the universal participation of citizens in national projects. We show that in some cases, a military defeat or a failure to keep pace with industrial development in rival countries stimulated the state to turn to education as a means of national revitalization to avoid losing power and prestige in the interstate system. (Ramirez and Boli 1987: 3)

Elsewhere, in unpublished work, Boli has extended this thesis by arguing that membership of a nation-state system is advantageous to the organization of the nation-state in its quest for stability and authority. Such a system provides a regulated environment for international relations and, by effectively separating internal issues from international concerns, the government of the nation-state can actually strengthen its legitimacy through lessening the importance of internal politics. Without the existence of powerful and stable states in a recognized state system the effective ruling function tends to be localized and autonomous, as in societies based upon feudal land ownership, but with centralized government on a consistent basis local government becomes relegated to the subordinate level. Michael Mann (1993: 479) extends this point succinctly by stating that, with the rise of modern nation-state administration, 'people could not return to their normal historical practice of ignoring the state'. The virtual worldwide adoption of the Western nation-state model has produced in principle a much more universalized relationship between the individual and the state, and the removal or lessening in importance of particularized local relationships between ruler and ruled. Furthermore, inasmuch as nation-states have adopted similar Western institutions in order to enhance their authority, as in the example of mass education described above, the experience of the individual in relation to such institutions has become much more similar, in form if not in quality. John A. Hall takes the argument a stage further, to the level of the nation-state system, and emphasizes the dynamic of the process when he sums up the approach of classical social science thinkers. 'These thinkers in effect argue that there were different levels to their society, the national and the international, and that the interaction between them, largely of a competitive nature, brought in its train human progress' (Hall 1985: 15). It is an example of a universalizing influence in the sense used in earlier chapters, and it applies despite the obvious differences in wealth and standards of living between both nation-states and the individuals within them. In fact, feelings of deprivation in respect of the range of citizenship benefits are one of the key distinctions between the 'haves' and the 'have nots' of the world.

At the same time, Roland Robertson's (1992: 100) concept of the interpenetration of the universal and the particular should not be forgotten here. The relationship between the state and the citizen is one in which people, actively rather than passively, reproduce universalizing institutions such as mass education. Thus their influence is, in fact, sustained in particularistic social patterns amongst which universalizing influences are reproduced. The routine of the school day exists for children all over the world and yet the institutions of the schoolroom, the timetable of lessons, the syllabus, and so on are reproduced with aspects of local culture built into them. This kind of process can also be seen in other, very different aspects of Western globalization, even where the social patterns are very clearly defined as, for instance, in the case of international diplomacy. Extremely precise protocols have been established for the conduct of communications and relationships between official diplomatic representatives of nation-states, through their embassies, consulates, legations and commissions. Yet, quite clearly, it is through the way in which such institutions and practices are reproduced by individual politicians and diplomats that the degree of change in inter-state relations can be perceived. The routine and the dramatic aspects of international relations take place in this way.

The relationship between the appropriation of territorial space by the state and the extension of inter-state connections appears to be inherent in the very existence of states and the state system. In the case of pre-modern city-states, Paul Hohenberg and Lynn Hollen Lees (1985: 22), following Robert Lopez (1963: 27), write of 'a paradox [in which] the city closes itself off from the rural environment in order to enlarge the scope and intensity of communication with the wider world'. The city walls form the container of 'civilization', enclosing and shutting off from the rural hinterland knowledge, wealth, and power, but at the same time reaching out to other similar pockets of civilization through long-distance trade, political representation, religious conversion, and military conquest. However, city-states could only maintain their power, authority and administration on any kind of permanent basis within the city walls, whereas the nation-state, through its much greater administrative and military power, is able to maintain permanent national borders around much greater areas of territory. Within these 'national' borders, state administration is powerful and effective enough to maintain authority, and the argument here is that the existence of a system of similarly constituted and empowered states adds to that authority through the collective value of the model within such a system – the nation-state system.

Therefore, I propose, the development of the nation-state system has produced forms of universalization in the relationship between the individual and the state. In the modern era the experience of the individual has been dominated by the nation-state as a particular focus of power in a segmented system of nation-states. Beyond this I would argue that, with the full realization of globalization in late modernity, the focus of nation-state power has been somewhat eroded by the direct influence of global institutions on the individual. The universalities of nation-state citizenship become supplemented by further sets of universalities emanating from other global institutions. Boli, in the unpublished work referred to above, sums up the processes involved as, first, the emergence of a global model of the nation-state and, secondly, as the increasing evidence for notions of world citizenship. The latter is seen as part of the erosion of the nation-state and in effect as a political dimension to globalization. Boli takes, as the chief implication of world society, the proposition that the individual as 'world citizen' is encouraged by normative influences to regard particularistic institutions as secondary. He goes on to suggest that the best-known and most pervasive example of this is the Universal Declaration of Human Rights. Moreover, putting the ideal and the material together, he concludes that, given contemporary levels of education, economic exchange and technology, world citizenship is meaningful in the sense that the average individual is capable of participating in global systems wherever they occur – which is everywhere. This is a position close to that of Anthony

Giddens, who in recent works (1991, 1992) has written of the emergence of 'life politics', the quest for individual fulfilment, as the successor in late modernity to the struggles for social emancipation during the nineteenth and early to mid-twentieth centuries. I shall take this up again later in this chapter and more extensively in chapter 7, on global social movements. Boli describes the material aspects of this development in terms of the global cultural flows discussed in chapter 2. These are seen as both desirable, because they represent the more attractive aspects of social development, and sinister, because they destroy local culture. His examples of these phenomena are the familiar ones of popular music, film and television, magazines, the novel, forms of language (especially English), and so on. He also includes those products which have become icons of global culture – Coca Cola and its competitors, transistor receivers and personal stereos, fashion clothes (with designer labels), personal adornments such as wristwatches, and fast food. However, the emphasis in this chapter should continue to be on 'world citizenship' and 'life politics'; the material aspects of global culture will be pursued further in chapter 4. I shall now therefore discuss the role of the state in relationships between the individual and global institutions, where its power may be seen as declining.

The declining role of the nation-state?

In his treatment of modernity, Peter Wagner (1994) writes of two crises. The first was when existence for the individual in modernity could no longer be sustained by the positive individual spirit of enlightenment and enterprise which had characterized the first social transformations from the inertia of traditional society. Instead, human existence needed help from established 'expert' forms of social knowledge. Above all this knowledge came from the apparatus of the (welfare) state, albeit the form of this was consistently debated and in dispute. The second crisis is that familiar to late modernity in which the authority of expert knowledge and of state provision are equally in doubt and the individual looks increasingly to forms of self-fulfilment. As Wagner (p. 176) puts it, 'terms like disorganization or pluralization appear plausible, since highly organized and bounded practices lose coherence and open up. While some practices of allocation and of signification are effectively globalized, others, some authoritative practices in particular, appear to be losing reach and coverage.' Wagner's point here is that, while the organization of communication, production and consumption progresses on a global basis, the organization of the polity in the form of the nation-state is losing its authority in the face of global communication and the global economy. The contribution of Ding-Xin Zhao and John A. Hall (1994) in examining the role of the state in social development advances this discussion by suggesting what form the state needs to take in order to maximize social development in contemporary conditions. In so doing they shed more light on the definition of the state in late modernity. In one sense they analyse what the state typically lacks in the societies of the West by comparison with the example of East Asia's economic challenge. They do this to define what form the state needs to take in a less developed country, given that all states are subject to globalizing influences of communication and economy. Their conclusion is that all cases of newly industrializing societies have in common the role of the state in potentiating participation in global communications and the global economy. Rather than directing the economy, as in the case of examples of industrial nationalization in Europe or the extreme case of the Soviet command economy, the state in the East Asian countries has merely operated enabling policies towards those elements of civil society which put themselves forwards for and show signs of global economic success. Economic growth has been made possible by high rates of investment supported by high levels of savings and competitive exchange rates with far-reaching support for education, training and the physical infrastructure. Instead of constituting an alternative to enterprise in the form, broadly, of the welfare state, the state potentiates and rewards enterprise. This is of course the rallying-cry of all opponents of the welfare state, especially those who associate it with the 'decline of the West'. This, however, is not the place for exploring that particular debate, except to say that opposition to the welfare state has not been restricted to any one nation-state. As an influence it has been carried internationally.

Moving from the examination of state policy in the face of global institutions to the dimensions of inter-state connections, Jan Aart Scholte (1993: 44–6) draws our attention to ways in which nation-states have given rise to new forms of 'transnational institutional link'. Diplomatic links, he recognizes, have existed since the Congress of Vienna in 1814–15, and were part of the development of the nation-state and the global nation-state system. However, more recently there has been a growth in intergovernmental links between what he describes as the 'domestic' ministries of 'justice, finance, health and the like'. Local government too has increasingly instituted its own forms of 'foreign policy' and these have in effect formed new international pathways, new threads to the global political network. In fact when this is taken together with the increasing importance of forms of supra-national organization – characterized perfectly by the European Union but also to a lesser extent by attempts to form common economic links in North America, across East Asia or around the Pacific Rim – then the precise status of the nation-state is put into question. The paradox is that in broad terms the nation-state remains the international model. As Maurice Roche (1992: 191) observes, 'Surely the reunification of the German nation and the emergence of liberated autonomous nations and nationalities in the post-Stalinist Eastern bloc and within what was the Soviet Union attest to the continuing strength of the nation-state idea?' The importance of this should not be underestimated even in the face of, on the one hand, examples of the corruption of the model such as the one-party system or, on the other hand, the alternative institutional forms at a supra-national or a sub-national level described above. Certainly the science fiction type of extrapolation in which the power of the giant transnational corporation eclipses that of the nation-state does not appear to be materializing despite the indisputable power that these corporations are capable of wielding in national economies. Only in economically weak and corrupt less developed countries have they exercised broad political power, while in the larger and more powerful states the role of the leaders of transnational corporations in national elites remains a subject for analysis and debate rather than conclusion. In fact the controllers of transnational corporations appear to have adopted relationships with the leaders of nation-state governments in which the two are mutually supportive. It is almost as though the transnational corporations need nation-states to provide a network of political systems against which they can plan their matrices of mass production (now in globalized production lines), mass communication and mass consumption. It is perhaps worth remarking at this point that the international organizations which have emerged to address problems of social development in the less developed countries, or problems of natural and environmental damage generally, have commonly been called 'non-government organizations' (NGOs) and not 'non-corporate organizations'. The implication is that nation-state government remains clearly and obviously the legitimated form of political organization, to which the NGOs form an alternative, while the transnational corporations are just as clearly economic organizations. Expressed another way, the essential Western distinction between polity and economy remains strong even at the international level.

Scholte (1993: 69) goes on to outline examples of what, using the language of international relations, he refers to as 'international regimes'. For instance, the Julian calendar is now some 2,000 years old but Greenwich Mean Time was accepted as the global norm as recently as 1884. The International Telegraph Union, which, as the International Telecommunications Union, now administers the all-important regulation of electronic communication across national frontiers, was established in 1865 and therefore actually predates the Universal Postal Union of 1875, although other forms of postal co-operation existed before then. Of other examples, the International Labour Organization is a remnant of the League of Nations, now attached to the United Nations. The General Agreement on Tariffs and Trade (GATT) has been a substitute for a putative International Trade Organization, originally envisaged as the third arm (after the World Bank and the International Monetary Fund) of the Bretton Woods arrangements. It has operated through 'rounds' of conferences to further the freeing of world trade from restrictive tariffs, but at the time of writing it is beginning to fulfil its originally intended role as a permanent organization. Such examples are legion and Scholte refers to them as 'international norms', accepting that there are varying degrees of formality and informality involved. He argues that they help to sustain 'deeper and more encompassing principles of social order' (p. 80). Social structures are for him 'vertical' frameworks which 'mark social order at a particular moment in time', whereas a separate category of 'social trends' consists of 'horizontal' regularities which 'organize social relations through time'. This is a rather artificial distinction and, as he acknowledges, other theorists see structure in terms not only of the passing moment but also in terms of the form in which social institutions are reproduced through time. As conceptualized by Giddens (1984), the duality of structure involves our understanding of past interactions, which we reproduce at the passing moment and thereby extend into the future. Nevertheless, Scholte's (1993: 83) references to what Michael Mann (1986: 8) calls 'diffused power' or what Steven Lukes (1977: 11) refers to as 'structural constraints' capture perfectly the way in which the kind of international conventions referred to here are reproduced in, and so form parameters for, day-to-day social activity. This is not to say that there are not reactions as well as conformity. Scholte's title is *International Relations of Social Change*, and of course the reproduction of social institutions by human beings always involves the capacity for change, great or small. With this in mind I shall now go on to discuss contemporary developments in terms of reactions to international norms. These take the form of emancipatory and democratizing movements. In late modernity they have typically had individualistic goals such as self-realization and self-fulfilment, or 'life politics' (Giddens 1991: 9). Life politics have been given greater potential by increased mass communications and contact on a global scale and, reflexively, in their propagation use is made of international communication and contact.

Emancipatory movements and the rethinking of citizenship

Arguably the most significant of the emancipatory movements in recent times has been feminism. The prime concern of the movement is of course the life politics of women and the relationship between men and women, but the pursuit of improvements in women's lives has had effects almost everywhere, albeit not to the desired extent. Spike V. Peterson and Anne Sisson Runyan (1993: 29) describe how feminist issues have not only been put on the agenda of most academic disciplines but have also 'altered disciplinary givens, challenged conventional explanations, and expanded the reach of intellectual inquiry'. As Fred Halliday (1988) points out, the outstanding exception to this, ironically in terms of the concerns of this chapter, is the field of international relations. It is curious that a social movement which, during the past three decades, has expanded through global communication and academic exchange should have been ignored by the academic discipline most closely associated with international studies. Peterson and Runyan (pp. 154–5) point out that, during the United Nations Decade for Women (1976–85), the Convention on the Elimination of All Forms of Discrimination

Against Women (CEDAW) was adopted and ratified by 110 member nations. Furthermore, at the end of that decade the Nairobi Forward-Looking Strategies for the Advancement of Women (FLS) was adopted by 157 governments on July 27, 1985. These were initiatives to improve the global participation of women at all levels and another meeting to assess the progress of the FLS took place in Beijing in 1995. The highlighting of these events is part of Peterson and Runyan's reminder that in the global society of late modernity all manner of social relationships need to be reworked and that gender relationships and the nature of gender are central to this purpose. Most of all the 'ungendering' of global economics, politics and the military at all levels from that of the individual to that of the global organization is a priority. They describe how this is entwined with other emancipatory movements of life politics, especially those of peace and ecology. As people reassess their relationship to the state and their associated allegiances, including military service, as they reassess patterns of production and consumption in the light of environmental concerns, existing definitions of gender which reflect a whole range of human strengths and sensitivities come into question.

Peter Beyer (1994) also addresses the range of a person's allegiances and attachments, of which nationality is only one. His emphasis is on examples such as the New Christian Right in the United States, the Liberation Theology Movement in Latin America and the Islamic Revolution in Iran, but each of these impinges on the contemporary issue of sub-national and supra-national alternatives to the nation-state. Despite the global nature of the nation-state model, nation-states currently have problems with non-state particularisms, or what Beyer refers to as 'socio-cultural particularism in a global society'. His main thesis, therefore, is that 'we should expect religiously based social movements focused on what [he calls] the "residual" problems of globalizing systems to be a persistent and prevalent response of religion – leaders, organizations, adherents – to this circumstance' (p. 97). The leaders and followers of these movements detract from the tendency for religion to become a 'privatized mode of communication' by turning it into a 'cultural resource'. As he argues, 'these are performance oriented religio-social movements' and, inasmuch as they concern personal beliefs and the right to practise them, they must be considered as part of life politics in the sense employed here.

In his recent work, John A. Hall (1994: 148) has reviewed nationalisms in their plurality and observes that if all examples of oppositional or peripheral nationalism were to achieve their objective of a separate sovereign state, the number of nation-states in the world would be doubled at a stroke. Johann P. Arnason (1990) has also attempted a typology of nationalisms which involves patterns both historical and geographical, the desire to trace origins and the determination to possess territory. This reflects the necessity for renewed attention to time and space dimensions in social science generally. The creation of the nation-state is one of the defining features of the modern era, but running through this work is the idea that a key process of late modernity – globalization – is undermining it. It was thought that modernity brought universalization but, in Robertson's (1992: 100) terms, the interpenetration of the universal and the particular results to some degree in pluralism. Within the broad structure of modern social processes, differentiation and pluralism are therefore an essential part of globalization. It is widely accepted that there is no satisfactory single definition of the terms 'nation' or 'nationalism' and, as the foregoing examples illustrate, globalization gives rise to enhanced forms for the propagation of alternatives to the individual's singular identification with nation-state citizenship.

The nation-state and the internationalization of economic activity

The internationalization of economic activity will be dealt with at length in the next chapter, but there is a need here to outline how this immediately affects the nation-state. Maurice Roche (1992) draws our attention to the broad dimensions of the factors that weaken the nation-state. These are the internationalism of global capitalist economy (Mann 1990: 11), as in the case of the Thatcherite opening up of the British economy to global capitalist economic forces during the 1980s (Gamble 1990: 90), and the need for the creation of 'a politics beyond the sovereign nation-state' (Held 1989: 204). Roche's concerns in addressing these developments focus on the consequences for social citizenship in terms of employment policies, welfare benefits and the creation of new underclasses. In conceptualizing changes to the nation-state and citizenship the experiences of the people involved are all too easily forgotten. Links between people's economic choices and the globalization of the economy are easy to illustrate and the successful examples of the 'McDonaldization' of eating out or the 'Disneyfication' of children's entertainment were described in the last chapter. But if this is seen by some observers as undesirable we need to ask what kind of a society it would be which could actually forbid fast food or animated versions of imagination. Economic competition at these levels challenges cultural differences and the sovereignty of the nation-state. As a result nation-states tend towards combination so that the scale of political organization can keep up with that of economic globalization. The approaches of economists to the internationalization of economic activity, as in the case of Peter Dicken's *Global Shift* (1992: 162–75), refer to the creation of a global 'triad' involving the European Union, the North American Free Trade Area (NAFTA), and East Asia led by Japan. I have already mentioned in the Introduction that the combination of NAFTA, EU and Japan is known as G3. Dicken points to the strategies of market integration and 'new protectionism' in the creation of such blocs. He particularly cites the 'guiding hand' of Japan's Ministry of International Trade and Industry, and its extensive industrial investments throughout East Asia and elsewhere, not to mention similar policies in Japan's economically thriving protégés, South Korea and Taiwan. The Japanese, South Korean and Taiwanese economies have been described as 'corporate, planned and dirigiste' (Lamb 1981: 107), in stark contrast to the model of Western liberalism, yet the success of East Asian industrialization is an important example of the results of globalization. Western culture penetrated East Asia only against resistance from existing Chinese and Japanese empires but, subsequently, enthusiastic reproductions of Western economics have not only modified the originals but actually improved on them. There is evidence that the Confucian social mores which are prevalent throughout East Asia have played no small part in the area's industrial triumph (Kahn 1979; Wu 1985; Gayle 1986; Murakami 1986). In October 1994, a newly established International Confucian Association met for the first time in Beijing with the aim of boosting appreciation of the philosopher, born more than 2,500 years ago, but clearly still providing the central principles of primary socialization in East Asian countries. The meeting was chaired by Lee Kuan Yew, the former prime minister of Singapore, one of East

Asia's most economically dynamic smaller states. He declared that his experience had 'convinced [him] that [Singapore] would not have surmounted [its] difficulties and setbacks if a large part of the population . . . had not been imbued with Confucianist values' (reported in the *Guardian*, 7 October 1994). Singapore and Hong Kong, together with South Korea and Taiwan, make up the so-called 'four little tigers' which are now at the cutting edge of East Asian economic success with Japan, particularly in the area of new technologies. In passing, note that this book, although published in Cambridge, was typeset in Hong Kong!

Pursuing the idea of centres of economic strength, Josef Esser (1992) also uses the term 'triadization'. He refers to Kenichi Ohmae's (1985, 1990) concept of the 'Californization' of demand coupled with the 'Toyotization' of the production process, as the successor to Fordism and Taylorism in the transnational corporations' need for world products rolling off global production lines. The convenience of market introductions for globalized products simultaneously in three arms of the triad is clear to see and Ohmae envisages a world in which Japan leads Asia, the European Union takes on heightened responsibilities for the Middle East and Africa, and the USA leads the Americas. The optimistic simplicity of this assessment has its origins in the rolling back of the state during the 1980s and the notion of the 're-privatization of the world', especially in the face of the long deadlock then faced by GATT world trade negotiators in the 'Uruguay round'. The simplicity of the scenario is, however, doubted by Esser, who additionally and quite reasonably fears for the democracy of social relations in such a scenario. Nevertheless, given the clear market importance of each of the three segments of the triad, the transnational corporations' competition for production and investment locations has given rise to supra-national planning, as in the case of the European Union's peripheral grants. This has undoubtedly contributed to the removal of some decision-making power from individual nation-states. For a case-study of the relationships between sub-national, national and supra-national economic and labour market planning in the face of TNC economic power, see Dunkerley et al. (1981).

Robertson, towards the end of his study (1992: 184), also refers to 'the triadic division of the contemporary world (a Japan-centred East, a Germany-centred Europe, and a USA-centred western hemisphere)'. But he argues that, while this makes sense from a global

economic perspective, it is lacking in terms of political and socio-
cultural analysis. For instance, it relegates to secondary status the
'massive – but certainly not homogeneous – presence in the contemporary world' of Islam and also 'a large proportion of what is still
known as the Third World' (p. 185). Elsewhere, I have argued for the
Islamic countries and the resurgence of Islam to be taken into account in any contemporary social science analysis of the world
(Spybey 1992). Robertson uses Balibar's (1991) concept of 'world
spaces' to illustrate that a west to east cross-section of Europe
produces what the latter calls 'three major ethno-cultural constituen-
cies: the EuroAmerican, the EuroSlavic, and the EuroIslamic'.
Robertson's conclusion is that:

> in both North America and Europe, and, in a less clear-cut way, in Asia,
> extra-economic and economic factors are intertwined with the trend
> towards multiculturality and polyethnicity within nations and 'mega-
> nations'. More specifically, many, if not most, societies and regions are
> subject to cross-cutting and often 'contradictory' axes of ethnicity and
> race, axes which define the range and scope of the world spaces that
> such societies and regions increasingly become. (Robertson 1992: 185)

As Durkheim was concerned with *anomie* in the transition from
traditional to industrial society, Robertson is concerned with what
Touraine (1981: 2) has referred to as the 'lack of laws or foundations'
in the globalized society 'which is no more than a complex of actions
and social relations'. The nation-state together with the global
nation-state system was, politically, the central pillar of Western
civilization's modernization project and, when it is transcended, the
result is a tendency towards a globalized world society. Globalization
in all its forms comes from the rise of the West and the implanting
of Western institutions around the world, but the outcome in late
modernity is a set of global systems that are multicultural and
polyethnic in their embrace.

Touraine's point about the lack of laws or foundations in the
globalized society is worth taking up in the context of the
internationalization of law. Touraine was of course referring to a
more general definition of social norms, rather than to enacted laws
with full legal sanction, but the latter are the most specific forms of
social prescription and they represent attempts to codify social norms
and expectations. Therefore, their internationalization is important
as the concrete outcome of what can be agreed upon in inter-state

negotiations. Yves Dezalay (1990) affirms that nation-states themselves are the creations of legislators, and questions how lawyers have adjusted to the opening up of international borders as a consequence of the challenging of state prerogatives. His response is that demands for the services of lawyers have expanded and if anything the model of the large Wall Street law firm, meeting the requirements of large financial and corporate houses, has itself been internationalized if not globalized. In Europe especially, he says, the 'legal big bang' followed straight after the 'financial big bang' (p. 281). New generations of lawyers, therefore, have much greater resources at their disposal to cope with the spread of 'American levels of litigiousness'. But his conclusion is that, as corporate finance managers have replaced paternalistic capitalists in industry, the legal profession, too, has become more instrumental and has lost some of its concern for social justice. Gessner and Schade (1990) set out to review the definitions employed in cross-border legal relations and come to a conclusion similar to Dezalay's, 'that large American law firms are extending their operations to more and more countries around the world'. This is a development associated with 'the dominance of the English language and Anglo-Saxon legal methods in international contractual agreements and arbitration proceedings' (Gessner and Schade 1990: 271). Their chief concern is with defining the need for further investigation in circumstances where the lack of 'sufficient normative guidance of either a legal or a cultural nature' causes concern (p. 254). In other words, there can be little doubt about the existence of the phenomenon and attempts at definition should be directed at established practice. In their study they engage with the work of Niklas Luhmann (1971) in the proposition that, as international actors increase their cross-border dealings, there is more awareness of cognitive differences and increased readiness to adapt accordingly. This is accompanied by a tendency to place less faith in normative and moral precepts. Dezalay's more critical concern about instrumentality and the decline of concern for social justice in the activities of international lawyers can of course easily fit into this framework which, with further examination, begins to resemble Weber's distinction between the *zweckrational* and the *vertrational*. The loss of faith in normative and moral precepts coupled with increased readiness to adapt is surely indicative of the means-to-end, goal-oriented rationality. Perhaps by definition, international social relations require pragmatic negotiations, and the norms of conduct so produced are quite distinct from the kind of normative and moral codes which are sustainable in national cultures. Possibly the norms of an open global culture can only be viewed unfavourably from the certainties of a bounded national culture and this is what makes international relations appear so difficult and the outwardly successful examples of globalization, such as McDonald's, so vulgar and lacking in refinement.

The erosion of the nation-state and the shrinking of state power has been associated with the creation of global–regional economic blocs, on the one hand, and with a heightened awareness of peripheral nationalisms on the other. The global–regional blocs take the form of a triadization process involving the European Union, North America and East Asia. This, however, must be interpreted in the context of an increased role for the United Nations and other supra-national organizations in the political sphere (Crook et al. 1992). In November 1994 the UN convened a ministerial conference on transnational organized crime with a view to taking a greater role in combating international crime following its initiative against drugs in 1988. The media recorded Britain's opposition to this on the grounds of cost but also, significantly, of fears that it would hand the UN powers which 'rightly belonged to national governments'. There is also the more general issue of the loss of US global hegemony, since approximately 1970, both in political affairs, following the Vietnam débâcle, and in economic affairs, with the end of dollar–gold convertibility which was the cornerstone of the original Bretton Woods global financial arrangements. This has led some observers to speculate about an impending transfer of the focus of the global political economy from the Atlantic to the Pacific, with North America's economically powerful west coast included in a Pacific Rim of overriding future economic strength. In November 1993 there was a meeting in Seattle of the heads of twelve Asian and Pacific nations at which US policy appeared to be to persuade the states of the Pacific Rim that their future lay with the USA. Behind this was the obvious assumption that countries of the Confucian tradition would be the key to continuing economic growth in the twenty-first century. There was a further Asia–Pacific summit in Jakarta in November 1994 and it is intended that the meetings will continue annually with commitment to a fully fledged free trade bloc by the early twenty-first century. The scenario of Pacific Rim economic supremacy overall is, therefore, an alternative to the triadization concept, which has appropriate consequences for global politics and the relationship between the individual citizen and the nation-state system. It has to be said, however, that at the same time the USA has also, much less publicly, been courting the European Union and especially Germany with the idea of a North Atlantic Free Trade Area. Apart from anything else this would give the USA the 'extra chair' that it has always sought in EU policy-making. The world's only remaining military superpower, which for the past twenty-five years has been struggling against the erosion of its former undeniably hegemonic politico-economic position, clearly needs now to keep all of its global options open.

4 The Producer–Consumer in the Global Economy

The social science concept of a capitalist world economy predates contemporary approaches to globalization. Long-distance trade is at least as old as human civilization and in fact the exchange of goods and services between elites, in their protected centres of urban culture, is one of civilization's defining characteristics. It contrasts with the self-sufficient subsistence of the peasantry dispersed throughout rural hinterlands. Fernand Braudel (1984: 24) has argued that 'there have always been world-economies' linked with 'world-empires'. He is referring to the ancient empires which in fact only ever dominated parts of the world. Of a different order is the 'European world-economy' which became more dominant from the time of the 'long sixteenth century' (1450–1640). Immanuel Wallerstein (1979: 4–6) has made further distinctions between:

- minisystems – these are the social systems of 'very simple agricultural or hunting and gathering societies' with a complete division of labour and a single cultural framework – but they could only have existed independently before contact with a world system
- world systems based upon world empires – these are social systems with a single division of labour and a common political system, but multiple cultural systems
- the world system, a combination of capitalism and world economy developed as the capitalist world economy – this was centred on north-western Europe from the sixteenth century

onwards, with a single division of labour but multiple polities and cultures

As I have emphasized throughout, Western civilization arising out of Europe is unique in producing the world's first truly global culture, but here Wallerstein describes the process in his own terms, which are those of the capitalist world economy. Wallerstein made a major contribution to what Roland Robertson (1992: 65) describes as the 'global shift in sociological theory', renewing sociology's engagement with history from a global perspective. This holds despite the criticism which Wallerstein's work has attracted for its functionalist explanation of the roles of the core, semi-periphery and periphery in the capitalist world economy. Central to his work there is un- doubtedly an economistic–deterministic perspective which fails to recognize the full implications of the autonomy of the state and the developing state system in European civilization. Only in Wallerstein's more recent work (e.g. 1982) is it possible to discern what Robertson (1992: 67) refers to as a 'shifting away from deter- minism and materialism in the direction of voluntarism and idealism'. I offer the following cameo from the sixteenth century which was so important to the work of both Braudel and Wallerstein. It may be taken to illustrate some of the early effects of international trade dominated by Europeans.

By the sixteenth century, silver mined in Latin America was being brought back to Spain in substantial quantities and used to support the economy of Charles V's Holy Roman Empire, which included much of central Europe and Italy as well as Spain it- self. There was, however, a lack of commercial infrastructure in Spain with which to maintain this economy and supply the needs of the transatlantic colonies. Instead the commerce became en- trusted to a pre-existing European 'world economy' at the time centred mainly on the mercantile city-state of Antwerp with its entrepôt trade and substantial banking support. The silver arriv- ing from the Americas provided a medium of exchange which soon operated beyond Europe; one of the most striking illustra- tions of this is in the opening up of trade with China. Although there was much that European elites desired from China, the demand was not reciprocated by the Chinese imperial court. Silver, therefore, became a necessity for exchange and the level of trade was such that the Mexican silver dollar became accepted as currency even within China itself. This example of the internationalization of trade was an unintended consequence of the European conflict with Islam in the Mediterranean, which led to European maritime expansionism, opportunism and global colonialism.

The global economy of late modernity may be seen in a sense as a development of this, but in fact it is of a different order. The parameters now are the result of much broader and all-encompassing social, political and economic developments. For this reason, it is important to distinguish between the *internationalization* of trade, as in the example just described, and the *globalization* of trade which is a more recent phenomenon. Peter Dicken usefully defines this distinction thus:

> These terms are often used interchangeably although they are not synonymous. 'Internationalization' refers simply to the increasing geographical spread of economic activities across national boundaries; as such it is not a new phenomenon. 'Globalization' of economic activity is qualitatively different. It is a more advanced and complex form of internationalization which implies a degree of functional integration between internationally dispersed economic activities. Globalization is a much more recent phenomenon than internationalization; however, it is emerging as the norm in a growing range of economic activities. (1992: 1)

Next we need to consider further the relationship between economy and polity. One of the most important distinguishing features of the rise of the West was its constitution as a set of independent sovereign states, each acquiring overseas colonial appendages, rather that as a single hierarchical world empire. The independence of these states means that each of them participated in international trade and this gave rise to an international division of labour as people across the world were drawn into the production of internationally exchangeable goods. Out of this was developed the more integrated system of international economic activities which Dicken refers to as a global economy. However, the development of global systems in both politics (the nation-state system) and in economics (the global economy) has produced a set of situations in which other cultures participate on compatible terms. The European countries set up and thereby dominated the systems of global politics and economics in the first place and Western countries, especially the USA, still have a dominant role. For instance, the United Nations Security Council which determines UN strategic policy has five permanent members: China, France, Russia, the UK and the USA; three are therefore from the West. The G7 grouping of major economic powers, which was set up in 1975 as an emergency response to the OPEC oil price increases of 1973–4, is made up of Canada, France, Germany, Italy, Japan, UK and the USA. It is therefore completely Western except for the single case of Japan. Yet, once created, global systems are almost by definition subject to participation by other nation-states, particularly since all have emulated Western models of politics and economics and to an extent absorbed Western culture generally. Already the G7 grouping is in the process of being superseded for global economic summits by G3, which gives Japan, in practice representing East Asia, a proportionally greater voice alongside two other entities, the North American Free Trade Area (the USA, Canada and Mexico) and the European Union.

The European state system came into being to accommodate the developing constitutional form of Europe. Other nations have subsequently adopted the model, including Europe's former colonies as they attained their constitutional independence. Therefore, in its entirety, this has developed into a global system of nation-states which in 1945 was formalized as the United Nations. The international economic system at first simply consisted of international trade, but this implies too an increasingly international division of labour. From the sixteenth century this was dominated by Europeans and operated largely through the separate colonial systems of European states. During the twentieth century, however, the term Western rather than European has become necessary to reflect the rise to prominence of the USA. Furthermore, as other nation-states have gained influence, particularly during recent decades, the international division of labour has become much more integrated. Therefore it may now be accurately referred to as a *global* economy because it does involve global production, global trade and global consumption at high levels of interdependence. The division of labour, the production processes and the commercial exchanges have all been developed to such an extent that the terms mass production and mass consumption are now only meaningful on a global scale. Each has become integrated to that extent.

The contemporary global economy

In recent literature the concept of 'disorganized capital' (Offe 1985; Lash and Urry 1987) stands against Wallerstein's insistence that an organized capitalist world economy was to all intents and purposes the adhesive of the world system. It also goes against the classical arguments of Karl Marx and Max Weber which predict a progressively more ordered capitalist society. This 'disorganization' reflects the investment of capital and the dispersal of industry, finance and some related state functions amongst a globally integrated economic system in which all nation-states participate to some extent. Certainly the period after 1970 produced many examples of the breakdown of a relatively ordered system of economic exchange. Before that date the UN-sponsored Bretton Woods arrangements had provided the world with a financial system in which the various national currencies had exchange rates fixed with the US dollar, which was itself tied to the value of gold. At the end of the Second World War the USA had been the only country with sufficient resources to underpin such a system, but by 1970 the burden had become too great even for the USA. The implications of this can hardly be exaggerated. In the absence of orderly exchange rates, currencies have been made subject to continuous financial dealings on international markets and exchange rates fluctuate all the time. There are of course occasional officially planned devaluations and revaluations too. In 1973, only a few years after this fundamental change, there came the first oil crisis, which was precipitated by the Arab oil-producers' retaliation against Western support of Israel in Arab–Israeli conflicts. OPEC, the cartel of oil-producing and exporting countries, effectively quadrupled the price by restricting the supply of this, the world's most strategic energy resource. Not surprisingly it affected virtually all economic activity and the international market prices of a range of basic commodities went into a period of acute and unpredictable fluctuations.

This made people in the West aware of economic ills which the post-war boom period had tended to put out of the collective psyche.

Inflation in some Western countries reached levels associated with less developed countries and unemployment increased dramatically as industry declined. Some traditional industries that had already been declining in the long term collapsed altogether and failed to be replaced by new enterprise. New words such as 'stagflation', were coined to describe the combination of inflation and lack of economic growth, and 'rust belt' was the term for those areas where industrial decline was worst. Concepts of 'post-industrial society' took on a new meaning as the realization took hold that the decline of an industry in the West was often matched by the growth of one elsewhere in the world, especially in Japan and East Asia. This was reflected in the concept of a New International Division of Labour (Fröbel et al. 1980). In this context, Dicken draws our attention to Christian Palloix's (1975, 1977) explanation that these developments illustrate the third part of a clear historical sequence of three processes in the 'internationalization of the circuits of capital'. Dicken describes it as follows:

> The first of the three circuits to become internationalized, according to Palloix, was the circuit of commodity capital. This he equates with the development of world trade. The second circuit to become internationalized was that of money capital, as reflected in the flow of portfolio investment capital into overseas ventures. The circuit of productive capital, he argued, has more recently become internationalized. This is demonstrated by the massive growth of transnational corporations and of international production. (1992: 123)

From a sociological perspective this needs fleshing out a bit. The transnational corporations range the world in search of favourably priced raw materials and labour for production, and the finished manufactures too must be marketed globally in order for the maximum potential return on investment to be realized. Therefore, networks of supply, manufacture and marketing are assembled and at the same time these become matrices of 'profit centres'. The organization of global manufacturing is in all its stages an opportunity for a return on investment.

This is an idealized picture of course because TNCs are not actors. They are institutionalized forms for the productions and reproductions of human actors. Human beings, both within the TNCs and elsewhere, have created the means of achieving the general objectives described here through their actions in production and consumption. Such means have become institutionalized on a global scale. The export-processing zones in some less developed countries are an example of this. Transnational corporations need labour at 'competitive' prices and government ministers in the less developed countries need employment for their underemployed populations at almost any price. For some young women in Asia, employment in an export-processing zone is the preferred alternative, albeit an under-paid one by Western standards, to an existence of service to family without pay at all (International Broadcasting Trust 1985). It is not just the controllers of the TNCs that are involved in the globalization of manufacturing, but a range of actors in different combinations of social, political and economic circumstances. In fact, it is mistaken to separate culture from polity and economy, or even to regard culture as epiphenomenal as Wallerstein has done in much of his work (Robertson 1992: 65). It is reminiscent of the mistake in the 'post-capitalist thesis' through which twentieth-century developments in the 'divorce' of ownership and control and the 'decomposition' of capital and labour were taken to bring about a separation of en-lightened management from venal capitalist ownership. In fact, through the internationalization of the circuits of capital and the resulting global integration of production and division of labour, most people are now in some way connected with the global economy and its capitalist dealings.

At the other end of the scale from Asian women working in export-processing zones, in terms of proximity to the global financial centres, Sharon Zukin (1992) has described the artificially created cityscapes of Battery Park City in New York and Docklands in London. Each example is in its own way a social, political and economic construct of globalization. In this spatial context, Anthony King (1990) has traced the development of the 'global' city, particularly in terms of London's previous connections with the British empire and its relatively recent further integration with the financial workings of the other major global financial centres following the 'big bang' deregulation of October 1986. It is a development which interlocks with advances in electronic communications, and in particular computer networks, which will be examined in the next chapter. Jan Aart Scholte (1993: 49–50) has suggested that previous examples of such cross-border transfers in goods and finance brought about social change as in the case of clocks (Cipolla 1967: 7, 25), armaments (McNeill 1982: 241, 354–7), loans (Braudel 1982: 393, 1984: ch. 2) and stock market slumps in the late nineteenth-century depression of 1873–96. However, he notes that the process has become especially pervasive during the past century and he concludes undramatically but tellingly that 'the intensity of cross-boundary transfers makes it unlikely that a given reconstruction of the social order will remain confined to a single country' (Scholte 1993: 50).

By contrast, Paul Hirst and Grahame Thompson (1992) are not only more sceptical about globalization but also about the true existence, or at least prevalence, of transnational corporations. Separately, Hirst has set out his four basic requirements for the existence of a truly globalized economy:

> First, it would be determined by primarily international processes, rather than the differential performance of national economies and corporate and governmental elites. Domestic policies would be subsumed by open world market processes.
>
> Governments would become merely local service providers, like town councils, subordinate to the decisions of major companies and international markets. Interdependence and disintegration would go together, with the significant level of mismatch between governments and their conflicting interests in the face of international business pressures.
>
> Second, the main players would be truly trans-national corporations (TNCs), with an internationally recruited and oriented management locating production wherever competitive advantage and market conditions dictated. Unlike multi-national companies, they would no longer operate from a main national base. MNCs utilize branch plants and internal investment to overcome locational and governmental obstacles, but try to keep core capital, basic R&D, and the crucial components of value added in their home base.
>
> Third, globalization would signal a final decline in the political influence and bargaining power of organized labour. Capital would be internationalized and labour would remain predominantly localized. Capital rather than labour would migrate, rejecting policies that imposed above-average labour costs and high corporate taxation. Labour would have to trade down its social expectations to that minimum of provision requisite for advanced manufacturing efficiency.
>
> Last, economics and politics would pull apart. The global system would have no single hegemony or guarantor state. States that rejected the dominant logic of economic efficiency for national political considerations would lose out, and states that challenged the major TNCs and markets by threatening crucial resources would be subject to devastating economic, not military, sanction, enforced by private econ-

omic actors. The world would be 'industrial' rather than 'militant' in its basic forms of organization. (1993: 11)

We must bear in mind that what he is describing here is an ideal type for a globalized economy and accordingly, like Wallerstein, he is separating out the cultural aspects of globalization. His requirement for the existence of a global economy is an international system that is predominantly economic, governed by global market forces with national government or even the government of regional blocs, like the EU, reduced to the status of 'local service providers'. This ignores the consideration that the big companies probably do not want that amount of power. They appear to do quite well out of playing one political perspective against another for relative advantages of location, labour and market. This is not to mention the rather obvious advantages accruing from what has been referred to as the 'industrial–military complex' whereby large and profitable business has been obtained from the concrete provision for political, ideological and military conflicts between states and blocs of states. Hirst's vision of a globalized economy is just as illusory as Wallerstein's capitalist world economy in its reliance on an overly economistic perspective. If he is denying the whole concept of globalization because an exclusively economic form of globalization has not come to pass then it follows that he is ignoring the other dimensions of the process. The world is not a *tabula rasa* for big business, precisely because the Western model of the state is so effective and has become globalized. As Dicken (1992: 148–9) observes, 'It could be argued, in fact, that the world economy is today more, rather than less, politicized as the interdependence between countries has increased. Certainly, questions of trade imbalances, exchange rates and the like are as much political, as economic, phenomena.' At the same time, the view that the globalization of Western culture has turned the world into a mass of undiscerning consumers is equally partial. It has also created tastes and demands which the TNCs and other companies have competed to meet. Surely that is a large part of the explanation for the success of Japanese industry with its innovative technologies, its post-Fordist flexible production runs and its quality-control reliability. All of these are geared towards the fulfilment of demands yet unrealized. This is Kenichi Ohmae's (1985) 'Californization' of demand behaviour and 'Toyotization' of the production process – the successors to Fordism and Taylorism. For example, the *karaoke* machine is a completely created device, but it has succeeded because it fulfils many people's desire to sing 'pop' songs in public. Now it can be found in centres of entertainment all around the world – even in small and remote Chinese villages.

The transnational corporations in the global economy

The definition of the transnational corporation is brought into question by Hirst. He is apparently reluctant to recognize globalization unless it shows signs of a positive change in the way that the global economy operates. However, a broader definition of globalization and transnational corporations may actually be of more use in the critical analysis of global economy. His insistence that to be considered truly transnational a company must have no national base, while intended to do the opposite may well fly in the face of any intention to refine the analysis of international economic power. Some of the best examples of organizations with global economic power involve not only a clear national base but also very concentrated ownership patterns. Ford and the Ford family dynasty are often cited as the prime example of this (Herndon 1970). A much-neglected case is that of the giant, privately owned and very secretive grain TNCs: Cargill, Continental, Louis Dreyfus, Bunge, and André (Morgan 1979). The operations of these corporations are so extensive that, given the importance of grain in the human diet, they together form the core of the global food system. Furthermore, their reach is so great that they employ satellite technology to assess global supply as it grows on the prairies and steppes across the continents. Morgan (1979: p. viii) introduces them thus: 'The grain companies were involved in the well-publicized and controversial sales of American grain to the Soviet Union in 1972. But it was really only a year later, with the quadrupling of oil prices, that public awareness of the critical importance of basic resources deepened.' I mentioned earlier how the oil crisis of 1973 threw international commodity prices into turmoil. Being a staple foodstuff, grain is a central and strategic commodity by any standards and yet the share prices of these corporations are quoted on no exchange, the corporations publish no financial statements and they are broadly controlled by an oligarchy of seven families. They are certainly transnational in their impact on an integrated network of supply and demand involving farmers, brokers, shippers, millers, bakers, supermarkets and consumers spanning the five continents. But they would not fulfil Hirst's requirement for a transnational corporation that it no longer operates from a main national base. In this case it is a family base. Dicken defines his terms differently from Hirst by stating that:

> the term 'transnational corporation' [is preferable] to the more widely used term 'multinational corporation', simply because it is a more general, less restrictive term. The term 'multinational corporation' suggests operations in a substantial number of countries whereas 'transnational corporation' simply implies operations in at least two countries, including the firm's home country. In effect, all multinational corporations are transnational corporations but not all transnational corporations are multinational corporations. (1992: 47–8)

He goes on to qualify his use of terminology by reference to Cowling and Sugden's (1987: 60) simple definition, 'A transnational is the means of co-ordinating production from one centre of strategic decision making when this co-ordination takes a firm across national boundaries', and adds, 'This is not to argue that all the world's complex production networks are TNC-controlled – they are not – but to emphasize that TNCs play the dominant role' (Dicken 1992: 226).

Companies normally become TNCs as a result of difficulties in their export operations. This is often due to import restrictions imposed by other countries, a significant consequence of the operation of the nation-state system with fixed borders for the control of imports and exports. One way out is to set up licensed production in overseas markets and at some point to go on to establish subsidiary plants, either by take-over or by building entirely new factories with the latest equipment (Spybey 1984; Dicken 1992: 137–9). A sequence of such developments produces the transnational corporation format and, with the existence of numerous plants, various combinations of internal group co-operation and supply can be indulged in. The matrix of 'profit centres' referred to earlier is the aspect of this arrangement which allows different sources of supply and labour to be matched with different marketing outlets to produce the most effective combinations of competitive pricing and desirable profit margins. Additionally it must not be forgotten, as Dicken (p. 226) reminds us, that a transnational corporation 'also indirectly controls many of the externalized networks in which it is embedded'.

The background to the contemporary global economy can easily be understood in the following terms:

- the nation-state system is an arrangement for the government of defined pieces of territory containing designated populations
- nation-state governments set basic restrictions for the passage of goods and services across national borders
- the transnational corporation is an arrangement for the assembly of a network of production sites, labour sources and market outlets to make the best use of economic opportunities across the nation-state system

Increases in global trade during the second half of the twentieth century have quite clearly resulted in concentrations of economic development in three regions: North America, Europe and East Asia, Ohmae's (1985) 'triad' of global competition. North America previously involved only the USA and Canada but, with the formation of NAFTA in 1994, Mexico is also included and the grouping may soon be extended to other countries on the American continent. The European Union was extended at the beginning of 1995 to include Austria, Finland and Sweden (the Norwegians elected not to join) and in the future some of the former communist-bloc eastern European states may be admitted. East Asian economic success was originally centred on Japan, but the so-called 'four little tigers' of Hong Kong, Singapore, South Korea and Taiwan have achieved importance in their own right. Now the 'ASEAN-4' of Malaysia, Thailand, Indonesia and the Philippines, plus the 'special economic zones' of coastal China, have become economically significant too (Oman 1994: 57).

Since the Second World War the size of the global economy, measured in terms of exchange value, has grown significantly, although the rate of growth has not been consistent. The 1960s boom period, the uncertainties of the 1970s, and the 1980s recession are, of course, crude indicators of inconsistency. The size and proportions of the world's largest economies measured in terms of gross domestic product are set out in table 4. These are figures compiled by the World Bank for its annual *World Development Report*. This can be compared with *Fortune* magazine's periodic listing of the world's 500

Table 4 *Largest economies in terms of gross domestic product 1992*

Rank	Country	GDP (US$ m.)	% of world total
1.	USA	5,920,199	25.7
2.	Japan	3,670,979	15.9
3.	Germany[a]	1,789,261	7.8
4.	France	1,319,883	5.7
5.	Italy	1,222,962	5.3
6.	UK	903,126	3.9

[a] data refer to West Germany before unification.

Source: Adapted from *World Development Report 1994*. Copyright © 1994 by The International Bank for Reconstruction and Development/The World Bank. Oxford University Press, Inc. Repr. with permission.

Table 5 *The world's largest industrial corporations by sales 1993 (US$ m.)*

1. General Motors, USA	133,621.9
2. Ford, USA	108,521.0
3. Exxon, USA	97,825.0
4. Royal Dutch/Shell Group, Britain/Netherlands	95,134.4
5. Toyota Motor, Japan	85,283.2
6. Hitachi, Japan	68,581.8
7. IBM, USA	62,716.0
8. Matsushita Electrical Industries, Japan	61,384.5
9. General Electric, USA	60,823.0
10. Daimler-Benz, Germany	59,102.0

Source: *Fortune International* magazine, 26 July 1993. © 1993 Time Inc. All rights reserved.

largest industrial corporations, the top ten of which are set out in table 5. Such large figures are of course difficult to get into perspective, but the scale of the largest national economies in table 4 can be roughly compared with the scale of the largest industrial corporations in table 5. At this point perhaps it should also be acknowledged that there are global economic activities other than legitimate industry. Various agencies estimate the value of trade in illicit drugs, for the USA and Europe alone, at about the same level as the global sales of General Motors, the world's largest industrial corporation with

710,800 employees. Jeffrey Robinson (1994) describes the 'launder-
ing' of drugs money as 'the world's third largest business', after oil
and motor vehicles.

One precise aspect of the globalizing role of the transnational
corporations in the global economy can be measured as foreign direct
investment (FDI), the amount of economic resources from one
nation-state being used to make investments of productive capital in
the economies of the others. However, it is difficult to interpret the
meaning of FDI figures because much international investment is
between core nation-states. For instance, throughout the early post-
war period there was consistently a preponderance of US investments in Europe (Servan-Schreiber 1968), but since the mid-1970s
there has been considerable growth of European and Japanese investment in the USA. Additionally there is, as might be expected,
substantial investment between European countries. Yet, by contrast
with these flows, inward investment into Japan has remained mini-
mal. As Dicken (1992: 51–9) points out, the dramatic post-war increase in the activities of transnational corporations is indicated by
periods, during the 1960s and the 1980s, when the increase in FDI
exceeded that of gross national product for any of the major TNC-
base countries. Most transnational corporations are of US origin, but
the relative proportions of TNC investment have changed. His data
for the 1980s show that Britain was still the second largest source of
FDI although at a level only about two-fifths that of the USA. Germany had grown much faster in this respect, with its 'economic
miracle' following a post-war low point, but its FDI figure was still
only about two-thirds that of Britain. Japan had been the fastest-
growing country overall and its FDI figure for the 1980s was about
four-fifths of Britain's or one-third of the USA's. A simpler but
cruder way of expressing this is in terms of the numbers of
transnational corporations, according to their country of origin, as
given in *Fortune* magazine's list of the 500 largest industrial corporations and shown here in table 6. This indicates that Japan has quite
clearly moved into second place to the USA in terms of overseas
presence with TNCs. Additionally, there is a small but growing 'new
wave' of transnational FDI activity from the newly industrializing
countries. These principally comprise South Korea and Taiwan, with
Hong Kong and Singapore also in East Asia, and Mexico, Brazil and
Argentina in Latin America.

Table 6 *Distribution of the world's 500 largest industrial corporations by country of origin: top five countries, 1993*

1. USA	159
2. Japan	135
3. UK	41 + 4 jointly with the Netherlands
4. Germany	32
5. France	26

Source: *Fortune International* magazine, 26 July 1993. © 1993 Time Inc. All rights reserved.

The less developed countries in the global economy

In a subservient position to the triad or the NICs, there are numbers of less developed countries which operate export-processing zones. Such zones are part of the territory of a nation-state but the area is excluded from normal taxation or customs and excise duties so that foreign companies can bring in goods for processing and take them out again, at a low cost in terms of wages and similar expenses. The advantage to the host country is the employment of labour that would otherwise not have work and to the foreign company there is the attraction of wage rates far below those pertaining in North America, Europe or, increasingly, in East Asia as costs there rise with economic growth. This, then, is the economic environment facing the transnational corporations. The triad and the global economic dynamics to which it forms a triple core clearly pose problems of analysis for Wallerstein's Eurocentric core, semi-periphery and periphery, although he has in the past talked about future alignments (1984: 141). There is still as much inequality in the world, with Africa hardly figuring in these arrangements except as a supplier of minerals and cash crops, and Latin America failing to 'learn how to learn' from the USA as East Asian countries have learned from Japan (Robertson 1992: 85). Parts of Asia, too, are excluded from significant progress, but the dependency theory image of a capitalist world economy permanently dominated by the West, only to be relieved by socialist revolution, clearly has to be banished from our considerations if we are to make sense of contemporary global systems.

It is broadly estimated that only a minority of the world's population can actually be considered to participate significantly in the mass production, mass consumption sector of the global economy and this is clearly of great significance for the global view. It is not, however, the whole story because large numbers of the people who do not participate at anything like the levels that are normal in the West still retain aspirations to do so and this of course affects their attitudes towards consumption. It also potentiates the effects of globalization as a set of cultural influences. Nevertheless the rate of foreign direct investment into the less developed countries has, according to Dicken's figures, remained consistent throughout the 1970s and the 1980s at only 25 per cent of the world total. Paul Hirst and Grahame Thompson take up the question of equity in the global economy and show global investment flows in relation to population. Their figures broadly fit in with those of Dicken but emphasize that, with only 14 per cent of the world's population, the advanced industrial countries of North America, western Europe and Japan take 75 per cent of global investment flows (Hirst and Thompson 1994: 295). Furthermore, they show that if the figures for the most important LDCs in terms of inward investment flows are added to those of the triad, the proportion of investment which benefits 58 per cent of the world's population adds up to 91.5 per cent of the total. This leaves only 8.5 per cent investment for the remaining 42 per cent of people in the world. In the light of such a ratio, their scepticism about globalization may be seen as directed mainly at the lack of globalized benefits from international exchange. Their chief recommendation is directed at the need for effective international governance of the global economy with the aim of providing greater equity. The Bretton Woods financial arrangements, as originally envisaged, were intended to address this, but they failed to bring about significant improvement and in any case were effectively defunct by the early 1970s. Now, Hirst and Thompson argue, new agents like the EU remain 'poised between the old era of national economic management and the new' (1994: 279). Moreover, the current plan to transform the GATT conferences into a permanent International Trade Organization, as originally intended in 1944, is for these writers only the replacement of a relatively open forum with a closed one (p. 301).

Charles Oman (1994: 19–23), an OECD economist, would seem to confirm this when he summarizes three overall points about the globalization of economy from his viewpoint in the official economic monitoring agency of the advanced industrial countries. First, he makes it clear that globalization is not multilateralism. That is, there is no guarantee that economic globalization will bring about the kind of multilateral trade liberalization that would benefit less developed countries. The reason for this is that it involves not only the integration of economic exchange but also the regionalization of the global economy, particularly in the direction of triadization. Secondly, economic globalization is what he describes as a 'centrifugal' process. It consists of the growth of economic activity across nation-state borders and in this respect it is made up of a great many micro-economic arrangements and interactions, involving even small companies in globalized arrangements. It is enabled and constrained by the actions of governments in the form of regulations and barriers, but it is also stimulated by developments in technology affecting not only production but the transport and communication of products and production technologies. Above all it is a form of development that has the capacity to 'disrupt entrenched oligopolies'. Thirdly, while economic globalization itself is a centrifugal process, the regionalization which it has brought about is a 'centripetal' process. As Oman (p. 21) puts it, it is 'the movement of two or more societies toward greater integration or greater pooling of their sovereignty'. In short, economic globalization is a dynamic process which has entered into the smallest of economic activities. Yet it has not had a significant effect on global economic inequalities despite drawing a more geographically dispersed range of peoples into manufacturing industry through newly industrializing countries and export-processing zones in less developed countries. Instead it has encouraged the formation of large regional economic blocs – the triad.

Forms of economic integration

I shall now turn my attention to the ways in which economic integration has taken place within transnational corporations, between them and, of course, across the borders of nation-states. It is particularly revealing to look at the differences between key industries. By this I mean that certain industries can be related to different stages of the history of industrialization and yet all have been globalized. It is conventional to think of the archetypal manufacturing industry of the

Industrial Revolution as textile production; in particular the British cotton industry is regarded as the driving force of early industrialization. But, with the technology fully developed by the end of the nineteenth century, it has been relatively easy for other countries to catch up with the West. Motor vehicle production on the assembly line is then looked upon as the equivalent industry for the twentieth century and mass production is the touchstone of industrial power. From the start Henry Ford's vision was of the Model T as a world car, produced and marketed everywhere. During the 1970s, however, as the decline of the older industries was becoming apparent in the West, another realization was the importance of keeping up with new developments in electronics production. Here technological progress has been very extensive and very rapid. The 'lap-top' computer on which I am writing this book is more powerful than the mainframe computer that was in use when I worked in industry during the late 1960s and which took up the space of a large, climate-controlled room.

The textile industry

Taking the textile industry first, nowadays most of the cotton mills of both Europe and North America are derelict and form part of what I referred to earlier as 'rust belts' of declined and collapsed industry. Newly industrializing countries in both Asia and Latin America have been able easily to undercut the older manufacturers in the West, while in India a textile industry which was supplanted by the British Industrial Revolution has been recovered in a new technological form. Textile machinery is relatively easily transportable and the export-processing zones in a range of less developed countries have provided sites for some of the older manufacturers to relocate their plant in areas of low wage costs. In addition, the poorer countries around the Mediterranean have provided an alternative set of sites, close to the EU, for Europe's textile firms. At this point the distinction needs to be made between the textile industry and the clothing industry, although they are of course closely linked. Textile yarns are mostly manufactured on a large scale. The process of spinning lends itself to economies of scale and yarn is now spun in one single process using a kind of rotor instead of Arkwright's and Crompton's spindles. In weaving too the former key component, the shuttle, has been done away with and replaced by alternative means of propelling the weft through the warp. Patterns which were once produced by means of Jacquard punched card systems are of course now linked to computers. Knitting machines, too, have been subjected to the advances of electronic technology. The textile industry currently exists in both the older industrialized and the newly industrialized countries, as table 7 shows. The clothing industry is supplied by the textile industry, but it operates on a very different basis with a greater variety in the size of production runs, reflecting the exigencies of fashion and

Table 7 *Textile and clothing production: some of the largest manufacturing countries in terms of value added, 1991*[a]

Country	Value added (US$ m.)
Japan	48,524
Italy	31,375
Germany[b]	18,716
France	14,905
Brazil	9,907
South Korea	8,560
Spain	8,000
Thailand	6,667
Mexico	5,741
India	4,710
Argentina	4,627
Hong Kong	4,377
Indonesia	3,853
Iran	3,512
Belgium–Luxembourg	3,030
Turkey	2,961
Australia	2,640
Austria	2,567

[a] At the time of compilation no comparable figures were available for China, Pakistan, Russia, Switzerland, Taiwan, UK or USA.
[b] Calculation refers to West Germany before unification.

Source: Adapted from *World Development Report 1994*. Copyright © 1994 by the International Bank for Reconstruction and Development/The World Bank. Reprinted by permission of Oxford University Press, Inc.

taste as well as straightforward utility. Some garments, such as jeans, are produced in very large quantities for the global market. Other short-term fashion items appear in much smaller quantities but still the overall fashion market is global. Apart from a relatively small number of very large manufacturers the industry is characterized by a huge variety of smaller-scale operators, right down to the myriad 'sweat shops' which exist in major cities of the West and in a range of other sites all over the world. These various sources of supply are linked with retail outlets and it is the well-known North American and European high street chains that are in the strongest position to place contracts, both large and small, with manufacturers. Some manufacturers have become globalized through the establishment of brand names: good examples of this are Levi jeans, Benetton fashions or Lacoste 'designer' knitwear. It used to be the case that large retail companies expanded vertically into manufacturing but this is not so prevalent now. Electronic technology enables stock to be controlled and orders to be placed much more easily without the necessity for large investment in manufacturing plant. Some of the most successful examples of clothing supply during the past three decades have been small-scale, high turnover operations with relatively little fixed investment. When I researched the British wool-textile industry during the 1970s, I was consistently told that a well-organized cloth factor, with little more than tables and scissors, could make more money than a mill-owner with large fixed assets (Spybey 1982).

There are two points of significance to the globalization debate arising from this. The first concerns labour and is the virtually global belief that the 'nimble hands' of women are a prerequisite to the successful operation of garment manufacturing. The prevalence of female labour, not only in the 'sweat shops' where there is relatively little control over conditions but also in home-working or outwork, where there is virtually none, has been addressed by Fuentes and Ehrenreich (1983), Mitter (1986) and Phizacklea (1990). Elsewhere, Peterson and Runyan (1993: 160–3) assess what is necessary for the 'ungendering' of labour. In fact, of course, men have historically been employed in tailoring work and a more convincing reason for the overwhelming incidence of female employment is the low cost. There is a connection here with the introduction of electronic technology. This has brought down costs in many aspects of the clothing industry but while computers have been linked successfully to the machinery of spinning, weaving, knitting, pattern-making and cutting out, no really significant breakthroughs have been achieved as yet in garment assembly, sewing and finishing. This is where the 'nimble female hands' come in. It is relatively simple to set up small workshops with electric sewing machinery in places where it is easy to find women who are prepared to accept low wages for a variety of reasons. They may be unqualified for anything else; or they may be in a domestic situation which dictates that they look for supplementary income on a flexible basis or even work they can do in the home itself; or they may be young women in the developing countries, for whom even badly paid work in an export-processing zone is preferable to unpaid service within the family. Fashion designs can be turned into computerized patterns which are capable of controlling machinery which can cut through many layers of cloth. The next stage is assembly and sewing, and this is where a wide range of possibilities come in: typically they all involve female labour. Electronic production-planning and stock control is clearly a big aid in the assignment of work to various outlets.

The second point concerns the electronic technology and illustrates the way in which it can be a means to the globalization of specific approaches to the manufacturing and marketing of textiles and garments. Of particular interest here is electronic point-of-sale (EPOS) technology which permits instantaneous links between retail sales, stock control and orders to manufacturers. This is part of the electronic communications and computer networks which will be looked at specifically in the next chapter. A good example is the Italian clothing company Benetton which operates shops on a global basis. Each is linked electronically with headquarters, via satellite if necessary, and sales information is transferred daily. This is then collated into market intelligence from which production plans can be drawn up and continuously amended. In another example, Levi announced in November 1994 that in some cases they had begun selling made-to-order jeans. Personal measurements are transmitted electronically to a Levi factory where a computer-controlled cutting machine produces bespoke pieces of denim cloth for sewing. In principle, with this system there is no need for any of the manufacturing plants or the retail outlets to be owned by the company which owns the trade mark and conducts the advertising. The technology can be combined with the kind of subcontracting organization pioneered in a range of labour-intensive industries. Operations involving successful brand names or 'designer labels' may be co-ordinated from a central point and contracts awarded to appropriate manufacturers, some with a close relationship and others on a more speculative basis. The large retail chains with their huge buying power also operate on these kind of principles in their relationships with manufacturers.

The motor vehicle industry

Motor vehicle manufacture is the strategic industry of mid-twentieth-century industrial development. The reasons for this are clear. In terms of labour and employment, motor vehicles are the product of products. The assembly line is so described because it involves the assembly of a number of components manufactured elsewhere: carburettors, braking systems, electrical components, and so on. The resulting combination of large plants and associated component manufacturers makes for substantial contributions to economic infrastructure and provides large pockets of employment. As I have mentioned, Henry Ford's plan from the outset was for a 'world car', a standardized product, made from standardized components in a process that could be reproduced at many different sites. This is the essence of Fordist manufacturing. Previously the manufacturing of engineering products had been carried out on the lines of craft production, without standardization, so that even such basic items as nuts and bolts might have to be made to measure. Sociological accounts of Ford's innovations have generally focused on the assembly line as a means for the control of labour through the extreme division of labour and the synchronized pacing of the many roles. Just as important is the standardization of components which allowed unskilled labour to be used. Ford combined the advances in engineering measurement and standardization, pioneered by such people as Whitworth, with the scientific management of Taylor. The effects have been colossally significant in terms not only of industrial development and conditions of work but also of consumerism and the way that people live. Motor vehicles have of course changed mobility patterns, and the many other products manufactured in a similar way have changed people's expectations and lifestyles in general.

Ford began building plants in other countries only a few years after the first US plant, which was producing extensively by 1910. The great rival, General Motors, extended internationally by taking over other firms and bringing them into line, such as Vauxhall in England

and Opel in Germany during the 1920s. Until the 1970s, the time of economic reassessment emphasized earlier, the world car industry tended to work on the basis of North American plants producing the large cars which were favoured there; European plants produced cars for European countries and to a certain extent their colonial or former colonial appendages. Other manufacturers had to fit into this scheme of things and international integration was limited. By the 1970s, however, the situation had changed and the idea of a 'world car' had come back on to the agenda with the big manufacturers. There were several reasons for this. First, there was the oil crisis and a move away from cars with a high fuel consumption. Secondly, there was the realization that standardization could go through another innovative stage. This time the division of labour of the large single plant would be spread over a number of plants in terms of major components, so that one site might specialize in axles, another in gearboxes, and another in complete assembly. From this arrangement a network of supply could be formed, preferably with more than one channel for any strategic component. Apart from anything else this would circumvent the possibility of strategic units of labour holding the company to ransom by strike action as they had done from time to time during the 1960s. Thirdly, there was the growing competition from Japan which had progressed from a relatively minor producer in 1960 to a serious competitor by the 1970s. It was to go on to overtake the USA as the world's largest car producer by 1980 and now it produces more than a quarter of all cars built. A large part of the reason for Japan's success is a radical redrawing of Ford's system of assembly line production. Hence the term 'post-Fordism' has been introduced to describe flexible or 'lean' manufacturing with its implications for work and for consumption. Broadly, the principle is that the assembly line should work to fulfil demand rather than to produce a supply for which a demand then has to be found. Production runs are planned to suit projections of the market and more flexible technology, utilizing electronics, makes the execution of this possible. It was in these Japanese plants that the widespread use of robot units on the production line was pioneered. At the same time stockholding was cut down drastically by the introduction of *kanban* techniques. This leads on to another aspect, the use of subcontractors. The principle here is that the vehicle assembler should avoid as many ancillary processes as possible by arranging for the work to be done elsewhere but nevertheless ensuring that it will be delivered at precisely the right moment. The planning and co-ordination of this is heavily aided by computer. There are also *kaizen* or continuous improvement programmes involving the organization of 'quality circles' amongst the workforce and, generally, an emphasis on quality control. All of this appears to have been successful in ensuring that the end product is not only attractive but reliable. At the time of writing, the British consumer magazine *Which?* rates Japanese cars highest in all of its standard categories.

US and British car manufacturers have suffered particularly badly at the hands of Japanese competition. Chrysler, the third biggest US manufacturer, would have been driven out of business had it not had massive government support, and when BMW bought Rover in 1994 the last independent British quantity producer disappeared. Taking up the triadization concept again, Japanese vehicle producers have built several plants in both North America and Europe (Britain, Germany, Spain and Portugal). They were encouraged to do so both to create employment and to replace direct imports, which were a considerable contribution to the trade imbalances that have grown between Japan and the other two areas. Overall there is now considerable integration between Japanese and Western manufacturers, with some US manufacturers having a stake in some Japanese companies and vice versa. This, along with other cases of co-operation, adds to the globalized nature of the industry. In April 1994 Ford announced a further stage to its global strategy: its North American and European operations would be enmeshed and if that went well its Japanese associate, Mazda, would be brought into the arrangement. The aim is to create a smaller number of sources adaptable enough to suit the demands of individual markets but cutting out wasteful duplication. Elsewhere, there has been a spin-off from Japanese vehicle technology into other East Asian countries and, in a different case, following the collapse of the Soviet Union the mainly Fiat-built plants of Russia and Eastern Europe are to some extent seeing a revival with inputs from successful western European companies, such as Volkswagen.

The electronics industry

In each of my first two examples of global integration, I referred to the use of electronic technology derived from the archetypal industry of late modernity, the electronics industry. This is closely connected too with the contemporary developments in global communications which will be examined in the next chapter. If motor car manufacturing was the industry of industries during the middle decades of the twentieth century then the electronics industry is the equivalent for the last decades. Jeffrey Henderson (1989), in his study of the development of 'high technology production', describes it as 'a new mode of industrialization' and suggests that it demonstrates 'the global option' for the restructuring of industry in the face of the persistent crisis conditions of the past two and a half decades. Certainly if the two other industries described here yield evidence in their development of tendencies towards forms of global integration, the electronics industry was by contrast established on that basis. The technological breakthroughs came with the development of solid state physics in the form of the transistor which replaced the electrical valve during the 1950s; the silicon chip which incorporated multiple transistors during the 1960s; and the microprocessor which during the 1970s increased the capacity of miniaturized circuitry many times over. The pace of development has been rapid and the dramatic reduction of costs has rendered it widely available – a standard 16,000-byte memory chip capacity of the 1970s almost pales into insignificance against the 64,000,000 capacity normal by the early 1990s. But, of course, the application of the microprocessor is not confined to computers. Different versions are used in almost every composite electrical product these days including washing machine programmes, fuel injection pumps for motor car engines, and remote controls for stereo hi-fi systems.

It is generally accepted that there are five stages to the manufacture of microprocessors (Henderson 1989: 31; Dicken 1992: 321) and it is amongst these that we must look for the division of labour and the social effects. The most skill-intensive and capital-intensive stage is research and development. New generations of microprocessor are essential to an industry in which successive stages of development come so close together. Yet, typically, successive developments have competed with each other in different forms of application at different pricing levels. In the recent past R&D skills have been concentrated in key areas such as 'Silicon Valley' in California (the Santa Clara Valley) adjacent to Stanford University and UC Berkeley and 'Silicon Glen' in Scotland. Now, however, that pattern has been broken and there are 'state of the art' installations in a variety of locations including, especially, some in East Asia. The second stage of manufacture is called 'mask-making' which involves the production of the filaments which contain the circuits. This requires some of the same skills as R&D with the addition of routine technical skills. The third stage is the etching of the contents of a mask on to silicon wafers which are then divided into chips. Again, similar skills are needed but with the addition this time of some relatively unskilled manual labour for the more routine elements. The fourth stage, however, is the one which is most routinized and demanding of unskilled labour. It consists of the wiring up of the chips to electrodes which will form the interface with the finished product. The wires are extremely fine and the work typically has to be carried out with the aid of microscopes. This is where the skills of young women, both in East Asia and elsewhere, have been extensively employed with conveniently advantageous wage costs (Fuentes and Ehrenreich 1983; Mitter 1986). The final stage of manufacture is the testing and, as with stage three, all levels of skill are required.

This process of manufacture initially brought about a situation whereby, typically, stages one to three might be carried out in the West and the chips then flown out to East Asia for the labour-intensive fourth stage. The assembled microprocessor package could then be brought back for testing and incorporation into the finished product. But subsequently first Japan and then other parts of East Asia have developed the more strategic parts of microprocessor manufacturing. During the 1980s Japan overtook the USA to become the leading producer; Europe is still a relatively small source. The production of microprocessors is clearly connected with the assembly of electronic products in general, but the latter is more dispersed than the former: the production of microprocessors is concentrated in the global triad, but not so the assembly of television sets, for instance. On the other hand Samsung, the South Korean transnational corporation, has become the world's largest manufacturer of screen components for televisions including those assembled elsewhere. The electronics industry is more globally integrated than any other and microprocessor production is its most integrated part. Between the USA, Japan and Europe, acquisitions and mergers have been common in the short history of the industry and as a result various forms of strategic corporate alliance have been created (Dicken 1992: 330, 337–8).

Reflexive relationships in an integrated global economy

One of the most striking features of the late twentieth century is that in the globalization of the economy – with integrated global production systems, a new international division of labour and globally marketed products – the triad of East Asia, North America and Europe is clearly visible as a new triple core. Scott Lash and John Urry (1994: ch. 4) address the socio-cultural implications of this and suggest that each member of the triad has at its leading edge a characteristic reflexive relationship between economic effectiveness and socio-cultural resources. They argue that the Japanese model, the 'J-form', works on the basis of a 'collective reflexivity'. The post-Fordist flexible production networks which were developed as part of Japanese industry could not work without a social background of collective responsibility. For instance, *kanban* would not work unless the sub-contracted firms were as committed as the principals to the achievement of the overall goal. In other words, there is collective responsibility between firms as well as within them. Moreover, *kanban* also involves ideals of quality which have been approached through the horizontal organizational form of 'quality circles'. Horizontal forms with collective responsibility have a connection with Confucian or post-Confucian socialization which is clearly evident throughout East Asia and with the group ethos of Japanese society during the Samurai era (Murakami 1984, 1986). By contrast with this, the ethos of Germany, the leading edge of European industry, is seen in terms of 'practical reflexivity', the 'G-form'. This appears to stem from the Germans' well-documented respect for the practical and, especially, the technical aspects of work. This is something which, it has been argued, is lacking in British industry (Barnett 1972; Weiner 1981). Lash and Urry (1994) suggest that in Germany the technical orientation has embraced education, recruitment, management, unions and external support for industry at local and national levels – with clear advantages for technological progress and innovation. The key players in German industry have a 'hands-on' approach which is also generally valued throughout German society. Finally, there is the A-form, which is Anglo-American and is characterized by 'discursive reflexivity'. In the contemporary Anglo-American case, they argue, forms of reflexivity are discursive, in contrast to Japanese industry where they are collective and German industry where they are practical. By this they mean that those at the leading edge of Anglo-American industry appear to want to detach their activity from both industrial work and industrial workers. Progress is seen almost exclusively in the form of information systems and their institutional forms are characterized by 'science parks' where different forms of abstract, rather than practical, knowledge are embraced. Possibly, concrete manifestations of this are the current US overtures to the increasingly powerful Pacific Rim countries. Such an economic alliance could be expected to enhance links between US technological research expertise and East Asian manufacturing capacity. Already Western industry has allowed a large proportion of assembly work to migrate to East Asia while it retains the less tangible, more discursive side of production.

Lash and Urry's framework adds weight to the overall argument that there is interpenetration between global cultural flows and local cultural influences. The three categories form significant parts of a social development process in which recognizably different emphases in manufacturing, linked with particular cultural characteristics, have contributed to an overall global integration in production. At the same time, the mobility of people and ideas must not be neglected in the globalized society of late modernity and to this end Arjun Appadurai (1990) has set out 'five dimensions of global cultural flow'. These might be seen as cross-cutting connections with Lash and Urry's construct of the global economic triad seen reflexively in terms of socio-cultural resources. Appadurai sets out his dimensions because he believes that in the face of globalization we need to address 'certain fundamental disjunctures between economy, culture and politics'. The first of his dimensions consists of 'ethnoscapes': these are the landscapes made up of people who choose or are forced by economic need to travel the world to find work and income. Secondly, there are 'technoscapes' which constitute the medium for consequences of the international division of labour and the integration of production, as described in the previous section. There is clear scope here for links with what Lash and Urry have described as reflexivity between the economic and the cultural. Thirdly, there are 'finanscapes' which describe the integrated financial dealings of a global economy. A prime example of these are the 24-hour financial dealings on world markets in stocks, currencies and commodities which have been made possible by computer networks in the global communication system. Taken together, Appadurai regards these three dimensions as disruptive of the individual's perspective on society in a way that is curiously reminiscent of the Durkheimian distinction between mechanical and organic social structure and concern about *anomie*. Appadurai goes on to describe 'mediascapes', which are the many and burgeoning forms for communication and the dissemination of information, and 'ideoscapes', which are ideological messages relating to modernity and the various reactions that it has elucidated in different political systems. Lash and Urry (1994: 307) associate Appadurai's framework with the disembedding effects of post-modernity. Traditional social relationships become displaced by people's relationships through globalized institutions.

It is important to explore the ways in which globalization and the global integration of institutions have broken down old distinctions and inequalities and replaced them with new ones. This chapter has disputed the causes of global inequality portrayed in the capitalist world economy approach to globalization inspired by Wallerstein. It has done this by exploring the balance between, on the one hand, a concept of global institutions 'up for grabs' and no longer controlled by the West and, on the other, the machinations and contemporary inequalities of a triadized global economy. However, in further investigation of both the emancipatory aspects of globalization and its less desirable consequences I will now go on to consider the global communication system.

5 The Viewer in the Global Communication System

Shrinking time and space

Increasingly people are world travellers. Not only has tourism progressed in scope from the national, to the continental, to the global, but people also 'visit' far-flung places daily through the medium of their television screens (Hebdige 1990). Our perception of what surrounds us, 'our world', has been extended dramatically in time and space. In tribal society spatial movement was very limited, in the sense that even nomadic or migratory movement was collective and constituted a kind of moving village with a social structure that constrained the individual. In civilization, with its physical separation of a small urban elite from the rural peasantry, some people – the nobility, the clergy and the traders, with a few others such as pilgrims and mariners – extended the horizons of their perception of the world. But it has been in modern society – Western civilization, its 'progress' and its outcomes – that the mass of the population has become acquainted with the wider world through mass communications and travel. The technologies of the West have made it possible for everyone to travel but, perhaps more significantly, for messages to be transmitted through space instantaneously and independently of any human messenger.

During the late 1960s and early 1970s 'futurologists' began to talk about the 'information society'. They were extrapolating, in social terms, the effects that developments in electronic technology might have upon all of us, in terms of the collection, storage and dissemination of information – of a visual as well as of a textual or numerical nature. If anything, however, they underestimated the changes that became commonplace during the 1980s and continued into the 1990s. To begin with things close to hand: I am writing this book on a lap-top computer using a word-processing programme and I do this in common with many other people who are faced with the task of turning ideas into text. The typewriter is virtually out of date. The computer in question is little larger than the book which it plays a part in producing. Yet it has a storage capacity superior to the first computer that I worked with some thirty years ago and that took up the space of an entire room. My current personal computer is capable of being connected, by means of a 'docking' arrangement, to computer networks that embrace the university, the nation-state and, in fact, the world. For there are two main thrusts to the electronic revolution. First, there are the advances in information creation, storage and retrieval. Second, there are advances in communication via cables and optical fibres, or airwaves and space satellites. More and more the different aspects of the technology converge and the compact disc, for instance, can be used to store many types of audio-visual information. It has become accepted now that television, telephones and computers will integrate over the next ten years to provide interactive services ranging from home shopping, a high technology replacement for mail order, to virtual reality experiences of a much more innovatory nature.

In an overview of these developments, Scott Lash and John Urry (1994: 25) detail six principal 'media' of communication and I shall expand on these as follows:

- *Transportation* – for most of human history, travel and communication have been the same thing because there was no significant means of transmitting messages without the accompaniment of a human messenger. During the nineteenth century railways and steamships effectively freed transportation from the constraints of naturally occurring power sources. Today postal and express messenger services fall into this category but with much faster transport networks.
- *Wire cable* – the electric telegraph was first used successfully between Baltimore and Washington by Samuel Morse in 1844. This was the breakthrough which meant that messages could be

transmitted independently of travel and, amongst other things, the continental railway timetables of North America could be operated more easily with independent communication. The telegraph was developed into the telephone but, while wire is robust, the volume of information that it can carry is low and insufficient for images. Therefore better media have been developed as follows.

- *Coaxial cable* – this enables a much greater volume of information to be transmitted so that images (for example fax messages) and data (for example some electronic networks) as well as voice can be carried. It is reliable but relatively expensive to use.
- *Wireless broadcasting* – another major breakthrough in communication was of course messages without wires, the broadcasting of mass communications first by radio receiver and then by television. High-definition pictures can be carried but the medium is unreliable in the sense that it is subject to interference from weather conditions. Therefore it is not suitable for some forms of data transfer. Recent successful developments are citizens' band radio, paging devices, remote time-switches, improved mobile 'intercom' systems, and mobile/cellular telephones.
- *Earth satellite* – expensive to launch but the volume of messages is now high. The first 'Intelsat' satellite in 1965 could carry 240 telephone conversations or the transmissions of two television stations, but by the next century a much-developed system could be carrying over a million messages simultaneously. Therefore this medium has become cheaper to use; also, costs are not affected by distance which makes it suitable for remote areas.
- *Fibre optic cable* – rapid and very large carrying capacity (six-figure quantities of messages simultaneously). It is expensive and centralized, and therefore concentrated in the triadized 'global digital highway' between North America, Europe and East Asia. It is not viable for remote areas.

The first three forms of communication described above are associated with modernity and they brought about significant 'time–space convergence', and also 'time–cost convergence', but mainly on a national scale. The railways enabled not only daily postal services to become routinized but also facilitated the distribution of daily national newspapers. Each of these three forms was revolutionary in terms of travel and communication, but they were also all socially emancipating because they were or soon became cheap enough for anyone to use. The second three forms are the products of technological advances during late modernity and they have extended both time–space and time–cost convergences on to the global scale. They are also emancipatory because revolutionary advances in electronics and in the organization of the media have made radios, telephones, television sets, home computers and fax machines relatively cheap to buy and therefore widely available. For some time, especially in Europe, the conventional thinking was that there could only be one system of utility services like telephones, but now there is a choice contrived from the variety of ways in which signals and messages can be conveyed. With fibre-optic cables a range of alternative means can be created at a stroke by, for instance, wrapping them around the cables of the existing electricity grid system and so linking up towns and cities throughout an area of electricity usage which is virtually universal, leaving out only the least developed regions.

Two notable things are missing from the list of electronic appliances mentioned above: stereo systems and videocassette players. These are just as much a part of the 'electronic revolution' in so far as it has affected everyday life, and they point to a particular thread in the development of communications that is missing from the sixfold set of categories described above. During the early part of the twentieth century the means were developed to record sounds and to present the result in a convenient form for reproduction or playing back in the home. The record industry came into existence. During the same period the means were developed for projecting moving images – 'movies' – on to a screen and this gave rise to the cinema industry. Put together recorded sound and moving pictures produced 'talking pictures'. Films and popular music are for the most part leisure activities and are therefore prone to be regarded as less serious than the industrial and commercial uses of electronic technology. But they have clearly been very significant in the reproduction of Western culture during the twentieth century and particularly important in its 'distanciation' through time and space. Moreover, through the interpenetration of the global and the local, the universalization of the Western popular culture mode has given rise to many particularistic versions of cinema and recorded music. However, it is undeniable that traditional forms of entertainment have become displaced to a great extent by these archetypal manifestations of modern cul-

ture. The cinema and popular music industries have became economically, as well as culturally, important on the global scale. There
are clear overlaps here with the material on transnational corporations in the last chapter. For instance, in the record industry there are
now six large producers: Bertelsmann (Germany – RCA and Arista);
Matsushita Electric Industrial (Japan – MCA and Geffen); Philips
Electronics (Netherlands – A&M, Island and Motown); Sony
Corporation (Japan – CBS Records); Thorn EMI (Britain – Chrysalis
and Virgin); Time Warner (USA – WEA Records).

As Western cinema and popular music became global institutions,
they contributed hugely to the ubiquity of the English language
which is a globalizing medium in its own right. This was a process
begun by British colonialism but, subsequent to that, it was extended
enormously through the position of English as the language of the
USA and its media of mass communication. Consider the basis on
which international institutions and organizations might operate if
French or German had been adopted in the United States instead. As
it is, English has become virtually a global language. In numbers of
users, as a first language, it is surpassed only by Chinese and that is
through sheer weight of numbers in China itself. There are more than
1,000 million Chinese in China but even amongst these the desire to
learn English is such that a televised teaching course was watched by
nearly 100 million people (Scarfi 1992). English tends to be the
present-day lingua franca even in Europe, with its strong separate
language traditions, though the European Union is committed to
maintaining for its major assemblies and documentation a system of
cross-translation which becomes ever more complicated and expensive as the membership grows. In a different example, English is often
used at pan-Scandinavian conferences to enable Danes, Norwegians
and Swedes to converse with Finns whose language is from a different
group. It is also the official language for the majority of international
organizations, including OPEC, despite its Arab/Islamic background.
After independence, India had little alternative but to accept English
as its official language because it was the only workable compromise
between the conflicting demands of the many separate ethnic and
linguistic groups. Words from the various indigenous languages of
the former British empire, such as 'bungalow' from India, have entered the English language and are in everyday use. However, this is
as nothing compared with the assimilation of English words into
other languages. The French government, for instance, is alarmed
that currently the flow of English words into French usage runs into

tens of thousands per year. Language is the primary medium of communication and the English language is clearly the primary medium of global communication. Most international business is conducted in English, which is connected with the fact that most transnational corporations are US-owned, but additionally 80 per cent of the data stored on computer systems is in English (Scarfi 1992).

It is possible to construct a table of major milestones in the development of transport and communication (see table 8). There has nearly always been some connection between transport and communication, but through the development of the computer and computer networks this connection has become more subtle. All kinds of complex information can be stored on computers, including specifications and formulas for a variety of industrial applications. These can often be transferred through global computer networks at will. To take examples from previous chapters, the world's major financial centres were linked on a 24-hour basis after the so-called 'big bang' of 1988. Chapter 4 described how design and cutting specifications for clothing production can be computerized and the information transferred from one country to another, for instance from a developed country to a low-wage, less developed country. In this example, high-value-adding stages of manufacture, that is design and cutting, are transferred by computer network to a location where labour – intensive stages, that is assembly and sewing, can be undertaken at lower cost. In previously conventional processes of manufacture, when some stages of manufacture were carried out in one country and other stages in another, customs tariffs would be incurred. But it is difficult to apply customs checks to computer networks. With open telephone lines how can the nation-state control this?

Jan Aart Scholte (1993: 46–9) summarizes cross-border travel and communications as follows. Travel was, he points out, originally for religious, military and trading purposes in the main, and it was not regulated by passport controls until the 1920s. Moreover, immigration controls did not appear until the late nineteenth century when the European white settler colonies in Australasia and North America began to set restrictions. In a different direction, as Basil Davidson has stressed throughout his work on Africa, the European states' use of recruits and conscripts from their colonies in both world wars created a class of people from the less developed countries who could never look upon the Europeans or their colonialism in the same

Table 8 *Developments in transport and communication*

Period	Technology	Transport	Communication
Since antiquity	Natural sources of power	Horses Roads Sailing-ships Canals	Human messengers
19th cent.	Steam power Cheaper steel	Railways Steamships Ship canals	Regular postal services
	Electricity		Telegraph Telephone
		Trams	
20th cent.		Underground railways	Radio
	Internal combustion engine	Motor vehicles Aeroplanes	Airmail
	Photography		Photographs Cinema
	Sound recording		Records and tapes
Mid-20th cent.	Cathode ray tube		Television
	Space rockets	Space flight	Satellites
Late 20th cent.	Electronics	Computer-controlled vehicles	Computers Compact discs Fax machines
	Fibre optics		Multiple communications

way again (Davidson 1984). This gave momentum to the struggle for independence (see also Albertini 1982: ch. 1). After the wars these more cosmopolitan colonial subjects were supplemented by increased numbers of students attending the universities and colleges of Europe and North America, as part of the implementation of modernization policies. Further international exchanges were of workers as immigrants during the labour shortages of the post-war boom during the 1950s and 1960s. These often became permanent even if that is not the way that they were initially envisaged. Additionally there is the huge increase in tourism, mentioned earlier, currently producing almost half a billion temporary cross-border visitors annually worldwide. Cross-border communications are of a different order to previous forms precisely because of the separation of travel and communication. But, as Scholte points out, it should not be neglected that the absence of patent laws and copyright allowed the free exchange of written materials before the modern period and this must also have contributed to social change. With the coming of modernity, the railways were the first to make daily written and printed communication reliable; from the second half of the nineteenth century, cable communications made possible the existence of news agencies, organizations such as Reuters or API, as further instruments of information exchange. These are Western agencies and their influence in the formation of global agendas for news along Western lines must not be underestimated. News from other perspectives has tended to be marginalized.

Moving on to the late twentieth century brings us to the huge increase in the number of audio-visual messages transmitted throughout the world and the notion of a global audience becomes a reality. Reference is often made to television programmes such as *Dallas* being viewed in almost every country of the world. This was not a factual programme, but the implications of its cultural message can hardly be exaggerated. Additionally, it is indicative of the preponderance of material transmitted from the developed to the less developed countries. This imbalance is reinforced by the huge cost of producing programmes and other material that will find a global market. Only the large media companies of the West, which are transnational corporations, have the resources to put together the skills and talent required for this type of material. They do so with the knowledge that the programmes are sold to significant foreign broadcasting stations before they are produced. Alternatively these programmes may be collaborative productions between leading Western companies for their own use and for sale to less well-resourced companies elsewhere. The broadcasting companies of the less developed countries can never hope to break into this cycle of production except in very minor ways. Meanwhile, as the various aspects of electronic technology converge, the so-called 'information super-highway' between North America, Europe and East Asia embraces telecommunications and computer networks with the aid of high-capacity satellites and fibre-optic cabling. Scholte (1993: 49) refers to this plethora of communication as potentiating and accelerating such major events of social change as the collapse of the Soviet Union which swiftly spread to eastern Europe, and the resurgence of Islam, particularly in respect of episodes such as the *fatwa* issued against the writer Salman Rushdie. In a similar vein, the contemporary development of global social movements in peace, feminism, and environmentalism, which has been hugely facilitated by advances in communication, will be addressed in chapter 7.

Another consequence of the spread of Western culture casts some doubts upon the future validity of the thesis that East Asian economic success can be explained by the utilization of indigenous Confucian cultural traits in the cause of industrialization. There is now evidence emerging of the unwillingness of Japanese youth to continue to conform to Confucian values. Furthermore, even established managers in Japanese industry and commerce are demanding less deference to business leaders and are calling for more open expression of opinions – like their counterparts in the West. While speaking one's mind is seen as a virtue in the West, maintaining deference has been obligatory in Japan. Whether or not this tendency is significant at the moment matters less than the fact that some Japanese see it as so and want to do something about it. It is an interesting conjunction, from a sociological point of view, that Japanese economic success through the particularization of the Western industrial model should lead to the questioning of the very cultural basis on which such an advantageous transformation has been based.

Global paradox: globalization and localization

Other writers have suggested that the flow of information on a global scale has effectively eaten away at nation-state boundaries. Lash and Urry (1994: 305–12) take up this point and refer to Arjun Appadurai's (1990) concept of global cultural flows referred to in the last chapter. Appadurai's dimension of 'mediascapes' is particularly apposite here. These are the products of the electronic media of communication with particular emphasis on their cultural effects. Mediascapes are constructs with which people identify, alternative to the nation-state or nationalism, or any other focus. Imagery projected through television, the cinema, or popular music becomes available as a body of knowledge, as a style and as a *modus operandi* which people adopt and identify with. Lash and Urry (pp. 307–8) also refer to Kenichi Ohmae's view that the flow of information on a global scale is eroding national boundaries. Ohmae (1985) refers to the combination of a 'Californization' of demand behaviour and a 'Toyotization' of the production process, as the successors to Fordism and Taylorism, a point also taken up by Josef Esser (1992: 11). In this scenario the international division of labour, global production networks and Appadurai's mediascapes converge to form an approach to the definition of global culture. Mass production, organized on both Fordist and post-Fordist lines, becomes globally integrated to supply mass consumption, also on a global basis. It is subject to global cultural flows which provide sources of identification for the individual as consumer. Indeed one of the purposes of concepts of globalization, in sociology particularly but also in social science generally, is to establish the importance of alternatives to the nation-state or other bounded entities as the most appropriate definition for society. The collective – that which confronts the individual in common with other individuals – is subject to global flows of information which transcend traditional or conventional definitions of society. The reproduction of a range of social institutions, including everyday ones like dressing, or periodic ones like home-building, becomes more subject to global influences and less to distinctively national influences. This process should be seen as a trend from the particular to the universal, or the local to the global, but one in which any notion of slavish copying is not satisfactory as an explanation. Any reproduction of social institutions is an active process and must involve a balance between the influence of the universal and the particular. The former consists of institutionalized influences extended through time and space as globalized culture. The latter consists of institutionalized aspects extended over a time and space that is much more bounded, as in a localized culture. As Lash and Urry point out:

> Global programmes, even like *Dallas*, are read differently in different countries and places. Audiences possess skills in reading and using programmes, through talk in households and workplaces and through the use of the VCR. At the level of audiences it is inconceivable that there could be a global culture. Indeed in some respects there is an increasing contradiction between centralized production (at least in some respects) and more decentralized and fragmented reception. (1994: 308)

I feel that the statement 'it is inconceivable that there could be a global culture' is confusing, but with their qualification 'at the level of audiences' they clearly intend to convey the same point that I wish to make here. The global culture exists in the sense of global cultural flows but the effects do not simply materialize at the point of contact with receiving populations (audiences). What may readily be seen as globalized institutions, because of their universal recognition and reception, still have to be reflexively reproduced in practice at the point of contact. In the course of that reproduction skills are used which are already imbued with local institutions and local culture. This is the principle of Roland Robertson's (1992: 100) concept of interpenetration between the universalistic and the particularistic. It is similarly expressed by Appadurai when he observes that:

> The globalization of culture is not the same as its homogenization, but globalization involves the use of a variety of instruments of homogenization (armaments, advertising techniques, language hegemonies, clothing styles and the like), which are absorbed into local political and cultural economies, only to be repatriated as heterogeneous dialogues of national sovereignty, free enterprise, fundamentalism, etc., in which the state plays an increasingly delicate role: too much openness to global flows and the nation-state is threatened with revolt – the China syndrome; too little, and the state exits the international stage, as Burma, Albania, and North Korea, in various ways, have done. (1990: 307)

As I describe it here, once a social institution is globalized there is no guarantee that it will remain under the control of its originator nor that it will be reproduced exactly as created. Rather, the converse is likely to be the norm since global institutions are by definition in the ultimate public domain and therefore subject to the widest possible range of counter-influences and counter-cultures. An extension to this point is confirmed by Lash and Urry (1994: 307) when they observe that the images produced by global cultural flows 'may be used for oppositional movements, such as with regard to environmental issues. Some such issues will be highly localized, some will coincide with nation-states, and some may contribute to the assertion of ethnicity.' Globalization is an influence, a trend, a cultural flow, but it can never be an absolute universal since in order to exist globally or, to put it more accurately, be reproduced globally, it must impact on particularistic cultural influences. This reflexivity constitutes a continuing part of the globalization process. As Peter Beyer points out, this is also evident in the work of Niklas Luhmann (1982):

> Globalization, in the Luhmannian context . . . does not mean the inevitable, evolutionary progress toward a global spread of Western modernity. Such developmentalism is inadequate not only because the empirical facts negate such a proposition, but also because, from the theoretical point of view, globalization should have as profound effects on the former territorial societies of the West as it is having on other former territorial civilizations around the world. Up until the middle of the twentieth century, the West may well have believed that its successful imperial expansion of the previous four centuries was essentially a one-way street. Today this illusion is rapidly revealing itself for what it is. (Beyer 1990: 390)

John Naisbitt (1994) has argued that both nation-states and transnational corporations are facing the need to address problems at subsidiary levels of organization. Nation-states have been a cornerstone of the Western modernization project since the Enlightenment, but now they are increasingly challenged by alternative or oppositional nationalisms. Regions of Europe have sought to establish their own relationship with the European Union and, as the leadership has made strenuous efforts to cement the transition from Community to Union, the process has been jeopardized by the issue of 'subsidiarity'. The global flow of information facilitated by computerized media networks enables all manner of organizations to compete in effectiveness with established bureaucracies. The transnational corporations have in many cases had to devolve their organizational forms in order to compete with small operators who have become empowered by information technology. This, Naisbitt argues, is the essence of the 'global paradox'.

Lash and Urry (1994: 26) describe how in late modernity air travel and electronic communication create 'relative location'. That is, travel or communication between strategic nodes in a global network become dramatically reduced in both time and cost, but localized travel and communication, subject to the parameters of earlier modernity may be unaffected, that is restricted to surface travel and the telephone. This is a concrete illustration of the paradox by which globalization is accompanied by localization. What Lash and Urry are drawing our attention to is a form of cultural interpenetration in which the universalization of air travel and electronic communication relegates other means of travel and communication to the level of the particular and the localized.

Electronics and democracy

Observers such as Bernard Woods (1993) have suggested a democratizing potential in reductions of the dimensions and, above all, the costs of powerful computers with their huge and flexible capacity for the processing of information. Relatively inexpensive personal computers may be linked both nationally and internationally through computer networks such as the Internet system. Tables 9 and 10 give glimpses of the growth of such a system even in less developed countries. A particular development that can have escaped few people is the tendency for electronic media to play an important part in the socialization of children. It has become a familiar joke with older people that they need a young child to show them how to operate electronic equipment. As with so many things, there is a huge bias in this in favour of people from the advanced industrial countries as opposed to those from less developed countries. Yet any contemporary definition of the former must now take into account not just

Table 9 *Internet computer system: host growth by geographical region*[a]

	1 July 1994	1 Oct. 1994	Growth (%)
North America	2,172,232	2,678,288	23
Latin America and Caribbean	16,619	22,535	36
Western Europe	730,429	850,993	17
Eastern Europe and CIS	27,800	32,951	19
Middle East	8,871	10,383	17
Africa	15,595	21,041	35
Asia	111,278	127,569	15
South Pacific and Australia	142,353	154,473	9
Totals	3,225,177	3,898,233	21

[a] Numbers: points linked to Internet.

Source: Third World Network Features.

Japan but also South Korea and Taiwan and certain other newly industrializing countries such as Mexico and Brazil, despite their obvious internal social divisions. The effect is that most aspects of society have become imbued with the electronic revolution and, in the developed world, when we reproduce the institutions of society we do so routinely by reference to, with the aid of, or even via electronic means, however indirectly. But even in remote villages in less developed countries, people commonly sit around a communal television set receiving information that is patently global in form and content. In addition to this intentional reception there are the secondary but none the less powerful media like advertising which to some extent reach even the most remote areas. In India the Indian satellite television audience is subjected to competition between the Hong Kong-based Star TV, controlled by Rupert Murdoch's News International Corporation, and the popular local Hindi language

Table 10 *Fastest-growing Internet domains (third quarter 1994)*[a]

	1 July 1994	*1 Oct. 1994*	*Growth (%)*
Argentina	248	1,287	419
Iran	4	14	250
Peru	42	114	171
Egypt	52	129	148
Philippines	65	152	134
Russian Federation	322	734	128
Slovenia	574	1,276	122
Indonesia	54	120	122
Latvia	180	341	89
Turkey	1,204	2,000	66
Venezuela	399	657	65
Lithuania	53	86	62
Estonia	659	1,014	54
Thailand	1,197	1,832	53
Uruguay	101	153	51
USA	16,556	24,861	50
Mexico	5,164	7,641	48
New Zealand	14,830	20,578	39
Costa Rica	544	745	37

[a] Numbers: points linked to Internet.

Source: Third World Network Features.

station, Zee TV, which uses the same satellite relaying system. The electronic media are certainly reaching some of the poor people of India and it is having a cultural effect. Star TV transmits a diet mainly of Western 'soaps' and pop music, but the Indian alternative combines Hindi films with programmes about controversial issues in Indian politics and society. Most surprising of all, Indian state TV, Doordashan, easily outdoes the two satellite stations when it come to audience figures. It is not so much that India is swept by Western culture in the form of television programmes, but rather that it has adopted the media of Western culture to provide a mixture of Western programmes, Asian-origin versions of the Western television diet and specifically Indian-culture transformations of the pattern. Whatever the format, Western lifestyles and aspirations are an important part of the message.

There are clear connections here between global communications and global economy. There is nothing like an outright monopoly at the point of contact but the field is tending to be dominated by a few large corporations. Yet there are differentials in the take-up of the new communications technology. In Britain it has, in fact, been slow. Originally, there were to be two competitors based in the UK, Rupert Murdoch's Sky TV and British Satellite Broadcasting (BSB). In the event progress was so slow that BSB became insolvent and was absorbed into Sky. Clearly, the hope of the News International Corporation is that Sky will form the European arm of a cable and satellite television 'triad', with the anchor system Fox TV in North America, and Star TV serving Asia from Hong Kong. However, the established global systems, CNN news and MTV music, have also failed to make much of an impression in Britain. Latterly, home-shopping by satellite television, taken up with enthusiasm in the USA and in some European countries, has not made much headway in Britain. By contrast with this, satellite television has been introduced in some countries without the precedent of a national television service. For instance, Oman was, until the late 1980s, a closed and very conservative Islamic country, but since its introduction satellite television has quickly become popular and effectively brings the world into people's homes on a daily basis. Oman's ruler has threatened that, if this brings disruption to the social structure, he will ban it. But it is difficult to envisage anyone, however powerful, being able to ban such a compelling medium. Its independence, both in terms of transmission and reception, makes it extremely resistant to surveillance. It is also very adaptable, a factor to which the continuation of CNN transmissions from Baghdad right through the Gulf War gives testimony. In ways like this, the progress of electronic mass communication continues and it is not just confined to satellite television. As this book was being written, it was announced in the British media that optical fibre links were being installed in 500 Chinese cities – and across the former USSR too. The report specified that an optical fibre the size of a human hair could carry 80,000 telephone conversations or equivalent messages.

6 The Soldier in the World Order

Industrialized warfare

Until relatively recently military institutions were virtually ignored in
sociology. This is all the more surprising when one considers that
classical sociology's single most central concern was industrialization
and that industry has always included, as one of its primary if less
visible products, armaments and munitions for the military. In fact
military production has historically provided pioneering technologies
for industry: precision-boring for cannon barrels was transferred to
steam-engine cylinders; military vehicles and aircraft have been developed for civilian use; and missile and surveillance technology has
been used for space rockets and communication satellites. The social
effects of industrialization have links with military institutions at
every stage of development and vice versa. The term 'military–
industrial complex' is one that has often been used in sociological
criticisms of late twentieth-century capitalist industrialization, although without pursuing the actual military implications very far. Yet
it was industrialization and mass production that made possible
'industrialized warfare', that is armed conflict which relies upon the
large-scale supply of industrially manufactured items. Ever since the
development of more effective firearms the possibility of running out
of ammunition has been a vital factor in battle and arguably, since the
American Civil War (1861–5), warfare has depended to a great extent
upon the continuous transportation of industrially produced weapons

and munitions to the battlefield. Each of the world wars was fought on this basis and if, in the first, shell production might be seen as a primary strategic factor, in the second it was aircraft and bombs.

More importantly for the concerns of this book, the industrialization of weapons and munitions production has set global patterns for warfare and armed conflict of all kinds. Industrially produced weapons are distributed through channels comparable to those of other industrial products. Many weapons are now part of the 'global knowledge', not only from their military use but also from their portrayal in films or on television. Terms that are recognized everywhere include the Armalite rifle, the Kalashnikov AK-47 assault rifle, the SAM surface-to-air missile, the Uzi sub-machine gun, and Semtex explosives. Moreover, there is no permanent and effective control of the movement of arms internationally, nor any formal surveillance of arms trading. Individual nation-states carry out such controls to suit their own internal and foreign policies. Supplies of arms and even of sophisticated modern weapons systems become available to organizations that are termed 'terrorists' or 'freedom fighters', according to the point of view, as well as to the legitimated armed forces of recognized nation-states. The Western model of the nation-state includes the principle of a monopoly of legitimate violence for the state, controlled through the authority of its properly constituted government. However, in some cases, particularly in newly established states, it is difficult to distinguish the legitimate military from the opposition to it or, to put in into the alternative terminology, to discern the difference between government forces and terrorists. Indeed, the globalization of industrialized warfare has facilitated competing definitions to the extent that legitimacy, as it appears to the observer, may actually be confused by the existence of a multiplicity of military organizations equipped with comparable weaponry. In some cases the only difference is a formalized version of ideology and the crucial factor may be external logistic support from one of the big powers.

However, we should not lose sight of the fact that the largest type of military power, the 'superpower', represents a different category. During the period of the Cold War there were of course two such powers, the USA and the USSR, and they counterbalanced each other with nuclear weapons and other advanced military equipment. Other nation-states normally aligned themselves with one side or the other. The NATO alliance was established in 1949 and the Warsaw

Pact in 1955. A minority declared themselves to be neutral, as in the case of Austria, Sweden and Switzerland, or part of the non-aligned movement established initially in 1956 by India, Egypt and the former Yugoslavia. Some claims of non-alignment were spurious, as for example in the case of Cuba, since its troops acted as a kind of military proxy for the Soviet Union in several civil war conflicts, particularly in Africa. The main point, however, is that this dual hierarchy of military power, involving continuous competition for advantage and predominance, produced a great deal of military hardware for the two superpowers, much of which was passed on to others. Favoured allies received certain chosen items of state-of-the-art weaponry as part of overarching strategic plans. Additionally, the superpower rivalry caused a great deal of military equipment to become outdated and superseded for 'front-line' use. This was then commonly passed down to other allies, particularly in the less developed countries. The result has been that throughout the period of the Cold War, between 1945 and 1989, there was a growing amount of military equipment coming on to the international market. Furthermore, although the urgency has subsequently gone from superpower competition in armaments, with corresponding reductions in arms spending, partial disarmament has provided new ways for armaments to appear on international markets. It is bizarre to consider that, in the former Soviet Union, tourist flights in front-line jet fighters could be bought only three or four years after such technology would have been classified and secret. It is frightening to hear that relatively sophisticated weapon systems and even weapons-grade nuclear materials have been discovered for sale. Meanwhile the USA, as the only surviving superpower, has exhibited growing reluctance to continue its global 'policing' role and has continually attempted to transfer more and more responsibility on to the United Nations Security Council.

In connection with superpower influence and international relations in general, Arjun Appadurai (1990) makes some useful contributions to the debate on global militarism and the world order. He asserts that 'The central problem of today's global interactions is the tension between cultural homogenization and cultural heterogenization.' As illustration he suggests:

it is worth noticing that for the people of Irian Jaya, Indonesianization may be more worrisome than Americanization, as Japanization may be

for Koreans, Indianization for Sri Lankans, Vietnamization for Cambo-
dians, Russianization for the people of Soviet Armenia and the Baltic
Republics. Such a list of alternative fears to Americanization could be
expanded, but it is not a shapeless inventory: for polities of smaller
scale, there is always a fear of cultural absorption by polities of larger
scale, especially those that are nearby. (Appadurai 1990: 295).

This insight recognizes the presence of Americanization in global
influences, but it also addresses the dilemma of 'polities of smaller
scale' which feel their independence threatened from other sources
too. Amongst the many consequences of modernity are the tendencies which encourage nationalism and aspirations to constitutional
independence. This may be seen as a significant consequence of the
'Enlightenment project', in the sense of Norbert Elias's or Jürgen
Habermas's work. The wartime Atlantic Charter, the establishment
of the United Nations and the end of European colonialism were all
dedicated to the principle of self-rule. Appadurai goes on to confirm
the contribution of industrialized weapons manufacture to the problems raised by this.

> The world-wide spread of the AK-47 . . . and the Uzi . . . in films, in
> corporate and state security, in terror, and in police and military activity,
> is a reminder that apparently simple technical uniformities often con-
> ceal an increasingly complex set of loops, linking images of violence to
> aspirations of community in some 'imagined world'. (1990: 305–6)

This leads on to his comments (p. 307), quoted in the previous chapter, about the globalization of culture not being the same as its
homogenization. Globalization involves the use of a variety of 'instruments of homogenization', including armaments, which are absorbed locally only to be reproduced as 'heterogeneous dialogues of
national sovereignty, free enterprise, fundamentalism, etc.'. These
are the familiar dimensions of 'security', on the one hand, and 'terrorism', on the other. Appadurai believes that this makes things worse
by translating internal politics into 'debates over heritage'. Modernity and its trappings encourages nationalism but not necessarily
with the constraint of the stable nation-state holding an effective
monopoly of the means of violence as was intended. Appadurai
therefore presents a rather pessimistic alternative view of the interpenetration of the universal and the particular. He describes it as 'the
politics of the mutual effort of sameness and difference to cannibalize

one another and thus to proclaim their successful hijacking of the twin Enlightenment ideas of the triumphantly universal and the resiliently particular' (p. 308).

Jan Aart Scholte (1993: 69) puts the globalization of armaments and warfare into a historical perspective reflecting attempts at restriction. First he points out that scholars in the ancient civilizations sought to define 'valid grounds' for the use of warfare and the conduct of the 'just war'. In some cases these measures involved the prohibition of certain weapons, considered to be inhumane, some centuries before the modern codes established at the Hague and Geneva. Recent attempts, he observes (p. 77), have achieved relatively little and certainly have not produced a demilitarized world order. The lack of a permanent international authority to facilitate this, he suggests, contrasts with the determination to set up the Bretton Woods arrangements in 1944 as a protection against world economic depression. Rather, the arms trade is an important part of the global economy and there is no lasting effort to restrict the flow of arms to the less developed countries precisely because it is considered good business. Scholte is curiously optimistic about the future (p. 78), but the percentage of the world's population permanently under arms has been calculated at 0.5 per cent which is a frightening figure when expressed in total – over 27 million for 1992! In the less developed countries large numbers of people are drawn into the military in times of conflict and instability, often from the least developed rural areas. These then become socialized away from rural skills and activities so that there arises the problem of what to do with them after the cessation of hostilities. This was a huge problem in Nigeria in 1971 after the end of the civil war (the Biafran War of 1967–70) and the outcome in some cases was banditry and armed robberies. The succession of military dictatorships since has not diminished the problem and even more than twenty years later, in 1994, there was widespread evidence of murder and rape by soldiers. The New York-based Human Rights Watch–Africa warned of the risk of renewed tribal conflict if the international community did not do more to restrict the supply of arms. In Zimbabwe the guerrilla forces which fought the war of independence during the 1970s against an unconstitutional white regime, were to a great extent successfully absorbed into the regular forces of the post-war state. By contrast, in South Africa at the time of writing, the military wing of the ANC is proving more difficult to incorporate in a comparable way.

Concern for the individual

The question of who should be admitted into military service and who should not is one that has become more sensitive with the progress of modernity. In tribal societies and in traditional societies, such as those of medieval Europe, it was normal for all able-bodied males to be included without any formal military training, although specific skills may have been encouraged at all times, as in the familiar cases of sword-fencing for the nobility and archery for the peasantry. These are European examples but there are equivalents elsewhere. In Japan the cult of the sword amongst the nobility held the gunpowder revolution at bay until the nineteenth century (Keegan 1993: 45–6). The European absolutist states of the sixteenth to eighteenth centuries developed larger, better-funded bureaucracies and established the principle of standing armies, even dispensing with the reliance upon mercenaries. The principle of the 'monopoly of violence' applied not only to the concept of state-legitimated armed forces but also to legalized monopolies for the production of gunpowder, gun barrels, and so on. In the face of new military technologies these states also founded military academies and gunnery schools reflecting the need for specialized military skills. No longer was it sufficient to rely on the gathering together of nobility and peasantry for warfare, although in some cases this still played a part in principle even up to the recruitment drives for the First World War. The change was in terms of permanent soldiery, the origins of which lie in the French *compagnies d'ordonnance* of the mid-fifteenth century; conscription, also originating in France with the *levée en masse* of the late eighteenth century; and the establishment of a professional officer corps, eroding the practice of members of the nobility financing and leading military companies.

I have argued elsewhere (Spybey 1992: 97–8) that the question of conscription is part of any overall consideration of citizenship and the authority of state over individual freedom and its curtailment. As John Keegan (1993: 50) puts it, 'how self-defeating is the effort to run in harness in the same society two mutually contradictory public codes: that of "inalienable rights", including life, liberty and the pursuit of happiness, and that of total self-abnegation when strategic necessity demands it.' In fact broad concern for the safety and well-being of the individual is a revealing part of any polity's approach to warfare and the military. In tribal societies warfare was largely in the form of skirmishes between groups of tribal warriors with traditional weaponry. The conflict was normally terminated when one side was seen to be getting the worst of it, and casualties were consequently low. In the civilizations the use of body armour was developed but generally restricted to the nobility. The height of this can be seen in the high medieval period when knights wore so much armour that they had to be winched on to their horses. Later, armour was made obsolete by the development of firearms until the development of modern alloy metals for military vehicles and latterly for personal anti-ballistic body armour. The ritualized setting of human beings against firepower became established in military strategy for a time but the cost in human life became more and more appalling with the development of weapon technology. By the time of the Napoleonic wars in Europe battlefield casualties were high but, as mentioned earlier, the American Civil War aligned the industrialized production of weapons directly with battlefield conflict. Industrialized warfare reached its nadir for combatants in the First World War when military commanders who in other circumstances might be classified as clinically insane contrived a tragic mismatch of outdated notions of glorious death with the realities of military technology. Persistent charges of flesh-and-blood human beings against concentrated machine-gun fire produced deaths in battle estimated in total at 10 million, out of 20 million deaths caused by the war in all. The Second World War saw a change of proportion but an increased number of deaths overall. It is estimated that there were approximately 17 million killed in battle, worldwide, out of a total 55 million deaths, including 20 million Russians and 11 million victims of Nazi extermination camps. The reduced number of deaths amongst soldiers, especially in relation to the total figure, was to some extent brought about by the use of armoured vehicles and much more intensive air support. This has become a feature of warfare ever since. In Vietnam the proportional cost of munitions in relation to numbers of troops deployed was higher than ever before, in an attempt to keep casualties to a minimum. Even this was not enough to assuage revulsion for the war and public opinion, stimulated by the anti-war movement, was the chief factor which brought it to an end. Now it is normal for troops to be deployed, according to the conditions prevailing, much more carefully than before. Marines and paratroopers, without the substantial support of armoured vehicles, were suitable for use in the landings for Britain's repossession of the Falkland Islands in 1982, but they were not appropriate for deployment against tanks in the open desert terrain of the Gulf War of 1990–1. More generally, United Nations peacekeeping forces now routinely use modern high-technology body armour, as have British forces in Northern Ireland and the American troops sent on humanitarian expeditions to Somalia and Haiti. It is perhaps ironic that in the nuclear age concern about the safety of the individual soldier has reached new heights.

The participation of women in the military

Another issue running through all of this is gender. The relationship between gender and the military and more generally between gender and violence is clearly a contemporary concern of global importance. Armed forces, either as constituted during the development of modernity or at other points in time and space, have hitherto, notwithstanding the Amazon legend, consisted primarily of males with females in supportive roles. During the past decade or so, however, the role of women in the military has been extended considerably – far beyond the few examples of women in combat in earlier periods. During the Gulf War there were an unprecedented number of women in the allied Western forces, in an equally unprecedented number of roles. This had been relatively more common for some time in the armies of the former Soviet Union and some of its East European allies, or in certain other cases, noted as exceptions, such as Israel. But certainly amongst the NATO powers and, it is fair to say, amongst most armed forces women have typically been assigned only to auxiliary positions. It was widely remarked during the fiftieth anniversary D-Day commemorations of June 1994 that women and blacks were virtually absent, or at least invisible in the ceremonies, and this is typical of any backward-looking approach to military activities. This is partly why the opening up of the armed forces to women today is so noteworthy.

Clearly the entry of women into a wider range of roles, including combat, is currently the single most important aspect of participation in the military. Spike V. Peterson and Anne Sisson Runyan (1993) have bridged feminist and international relations issues in *Global Gender Issues,* a book which amongst other things addresses this development and the broader issue of the 'ungendering' of violence. They first of all make the point that it is a rather obvious reformist strategy to increase the representation of women in the military at all levels and in all functions. This might not only improve the lot of women in terms of opportunities and the acquisition of skills, but also it 'would be consistent with the emerging goals of UN-sponsored peacekeeping and humanitarian relief efforts' (p. 158). However, they argue, while this 'does strike a blow against the stereotype of femininity' it does not in itself necessarily lead to equality either inside or outside the military. More importantly, it does nothing to bring into question the overriding issue of violence either in the institutionalized form of military combat or in its various domestic forms. Certainly the practical experience of women in the police and the military has not so far produced the transformations which, in principle at least, were considered desirable when the policy of extending access was formulated. Probably it is unrealistic to think that this could possibly be the case. Such policies have only been seriously in operation for a very short time and there are obvious levels of prejudice that have to be overcome in occupational roles so strongly linked with masculinity and violence. Peterson and Runyan go on to argue that changing the military in its treatment of gender differences is the same as changing any other social institution in isolation. The issue of gender roles has to be confronted in its own right and across all institutions, including those of international politics and forms of institutionalized violence. They put the most faith in the extension of global human rights movements, a subject which will be examined further in the next chapter. In particular they would wish to see a virtually complete redrawing of the UN Charter for Human Rights to incorporate the recommendations of the Convention on the Elimination of All Forms of Discrimination Against Women, adopted by the UN in 1979. They seek therefore to question the use of violence *per se*, regarding this as an issue which reflects masculine orientations and embraces international relations and gender relations alike. This is a distinctively feminist approach to the role of women in the military and it reflects the contribution of feminist theory to contemporary global issues.

The new world order

Soon after the collapse of the Soviet Union in 1989 people began to talk about a new world order. This is not surprising if one considers that the balance of power between NATO and the Warsaw Pact had been maintained since 1945 through the threat of mutual nuclear destruction and that all international relations had accommodated to that. However, the ending of the Cold War brought military uncertainties. What would fill the void created by the demise of the Soviet Union and the rendering of the USA to single superpower status? What would become of the stockpiles of nuclear weapons spread across the former USSR? Some were in the Baltic states which opted for full independence from Russia. Others were in Islamic states which have also become independent and are situated relatively close to militantly Islamic Iran. In fact, the Ukraine appears to be content to co-operate in the dismantling of the nuclear warheads located on its territory so that they can be transported to Russian nuclear centres for destruction. But the situation in Kazakhstan was to some extent retrieved only by the USA buying its weapons-grade plutonium and flying it direct to American nuclear facilities with airborne refuelling to avoid the need for stopovers.

The years since 1989 have witnessed a trend towards the increased use of the United Nations in international conflict both as a mediator and as a supplier of interventionist forces. These activities have not always met with conspicuous success, although the most intractable cases, such as the former Yugoslavia, are the ones that tend to be reported in the global media. I have suggested in previous chapters that the USA might be seen as having lost its global politico-military and economic hegemony around 1970. In politico-military terms the débâcle of the Vietnam war was the main factor, while the economic turning-point was the end of automatic dollar–gold exchangeability, the linchpin of the 1944 Bretton Woods financial arrangements. Subsequently, in the absence of any other superpower after 1989, there has been a significant change whereby the USA has been able to get unanimous backing from the Security Council when previously there had always been a problem with operations in which it would clearly play the leading military role. In addition to its five permanent members (China, France, Russia, the UK and the USA), the Security Council has ten non-permanent members elected from the General

Assembly for terms of two years. The achievement of unanimous support is therefore not an inconsiderable one and it reflects an important aspect of the changed nature of international relations since 1989. Security Council backing was forthcoming for operation 'Desert Storm' in the Gulf War, when several of the NATO allies plus Saudi Arabia and Kuwait were involved. But it has also been available for military expeditions in which the USA has acted alone, such as those in Somalia and Haiti. In a sense there has been a revived attempt amongst the world community of nation-states to make the United Nations into the (new) world order, as indeed the organization was originally envisaged. However, the UN always needs to have recourse to the armed forces of nation-states since it has none of its own, and experiences before 1989, when the forces of the major powers could not be used, were often unsatisfactory. It needs therefore to be added that the success of the Republican party in the US Congress elections in November 1994 may cause a change in the US government's approach to international relations. This seems particularly likely as the full extent of the failure of UN peacekeeping attempts in Bosnia unfolds and draws attention to the delineation between the UN as a forum of nation-states and NATO as a military alliance with armed forces to deploy.

Martin Shaw (1991) has made a tentative interpretation of the post-1989 world as 'post-military society'. But he makes it clear that this is not intended to signify a pacific society but rather one that has moved away from the nuclear 'brinkmanship' of the Cold War into a period of demilitarization. At the time that he was writing, what might be termed the Soviet military rearguard in Russia was revealing its lack of staying power as a political force to challenge the new form of government. There appears to be clear will within Russia to move away from military confrontation with the USA, just as in the West after 1989 there was an almost overwhelming desire to put the Cold War into the past, even when it was not clear exactly what was happening to the armed forces and the huge stockpiles of nuclear weapons. It could be argued that there is a great deal of cause for concern about the prospects for safely dismantling the Soviet war machine when so many other aspects of the new Russian society appear to be disorganized and subject to confusion and lack of direction. On the other hand the performance of the Russian forces in Chechnya during 1994–5 has raised doubts about effectiveness and added to the question of whether the USSR ever had the capacity to pose a real threat to the USA. In any case, in the West the so-called 'peace dividend' after 1989 became an added justification for the withdrawal from militarism and, although none too clearly defined, the promise of public funds for other more worthwhile expenditures has also proved a definite incentive.

Shaw (1991: 54) makes the important point that military force is in fact little used for long periods of its existence. Clearly this can be interpreted as a justification for defence cuts in a period of demilitarization. In the long term, with the development of wealthier and more powerful states, the maintenance of standing armies has created a situation where, unless warfare is permanent, the military spends most of its time preparing for war but not actually waging it. This situation is intensified with the existence of modern professionalized armed forces equipped with advanced weaponry because this depends upon high levels of technology and therefore requires considerable skill and training. Nuclear weapons, which (we hope) were never meant to be used after Hiroshima and Nagasaki, add to this overall effect. Consider the succession of nuclear delivery systems, by aircraft, missile and submarine, that have been developed by the NATO and Warsaw Pact powers since the Second World War. Happily these were never used in anger and after a certain period of time were scrapped as obsolescent – but only to be replaced by more advanced systems. Training in the use of these weapons, however, took place daily. For decades the USA kept its Strategic Air Command of nuclear armed aircraft in the air at all times. Radar installations across the Western world, linked via the US president with missile command posts, were manned around the clock. A similar story can no doubt be recounted for the USSR, although their situation is less clear to us in the West.

Even now nuclear submarines, formerly with Polaris missiles and now with Trident systems, are permanently on station, though perhaps at reduced levels of readiness. If the height of militarism was a state of massive high-technology preparedness without warfare, then post-militarism is merely a much-reduced version of the same thing. In reaction to defence cuts, the military establishment must be seen as striving to maintain a level of capability and establishment rather than as desiring to extend militarism *per se* – much less as keeping alive the possibility of waging a full-scale nuclear global war. Since the salutary lesson of Vietnam, the episodes of actual warfare, such as in the Gulf, have been relatively short-lived and the return to base for most of the forces is as rapid as their mobilization. The resistance of the armed forces to political demands for reduced spending is in fact largely commensurate with their long-term organizational forms and career structures. Colonels do not like losing their regiments and are quite capable of orchestrating public campaigns in their support. Admirals attempt to justify the fact that there are more of them than there are warships in modern navies. Technological superiority in equipment and the art of counter-politics against cutbacks are perhaps the twin concerns of the contemporary soldier rather than warfare.

At this point it is necessary to take stock of what has been set out above. Shaw's point about the lack of action seen by modern armed forces is a good one. However, if we stand back from his account, conceptually speaking, we might well come to the conclusion that it is an ethnocentric description written within and describing the core of the world order. It does not make much sense to talk about the military never going into battle in certain less developed countries. The unfortunate experience of populations in these countries is all too often of being caught up in situations where one militia is perpetually skirmishing and occasionally entering into full-scale warfare with one or more other militias. One of these parties may claim to be the state militia and indeed may have a good formal claim to that position. This does not, however, prevent other factions from disputing the issue. An example is the case of Angola. During the 1960s, when most African countries secured their constitutional independence from European colonialism, the extreme right-wing government of Portugal refused to grant such independence to any of its colonies in Africa. There followed a series of guerrilla wars and in Angola the forces of the MPLA (Movimento Popular de Libertação de Angola) fought the Portuguese colonial forces. By 1979, however, the junta in Lisbon was collapsing and a political swing towards socialism and socialist policies was imminent. With these changes the Portuguese colonial system collapsed and in Angola the MPLA found itself suddenly in government. It was and still is to some extent a Marxist organization, inspired by the liberation ideology of Amilcar Cabral, and it immediately found itself opposed politically and militarily by the right-wing forces of UNITA (União Nacional para a Independência Total de Angola). There followed years of fighting in which UNITA took advantage of considerable rural discontent in the confusion which has been not unfamiliar to the immediate post-colonial nation-state. Subsequently, even an open presidential election supervised by the United Nations has not brought an end to hostilities. The UNITA leader, Jonas Savimbi, was decisively beaten at the ballot box in 1992 but nevertheless refused to accept the result. The civil war was resumed and thus the unfortunate people of Angola have seen and continue to see another side to militarism and industrialized warfare. Until 1989 the MPLA was able to obtain its armaments from the USSR and for a while even had Cuban troops fighting alongside, as a diplomatically safe substitute for Soviet forces. By contrast UNITA, as an anti-Marxist force, was until recently able to obtain its supplies from South Africa and the USA. Now it is dependent on international arms dealers. Not for Angola, therefore, the situation of armed forces in readiness but not in action, and the situation has been the same for a number of less developed countries. On Europe's doorstep, also, it has become the case in the former Yugoslavia with its nightmare scenario of competing political and religious factions. These are other dimensions to the world order, relegated to a lower level of significance in Shaw's concept of a post-military society. But they are not at all insignificant in the lives of the people involved and the role of soldier and civilian becomes blurred when military conflict and its associated deprivations become the facts of everyday life.

Some of the more recent policy developments on the part of the big powers are, I think, a reflection of this. In September 1993 the US government officially launched its policy of 'multilateralism' or the internationalization of processes of mediation in international disputes. This allowed for the permanent assignment of troops and support to the United Nations for international peacekeeping generally and to NATO for the containment of disputes derived from the break-up of the former Soviet Union. To this end, specific training establishments were set up as part of the US military infrastructure, including a programme known as 'Cortina'. This was designed to simulate the problems encountered in places such as Somalia where US forces quickly became unpopular and lost the support of the very people they were sent to protect. As I have suggested, however, the 1994 swing to Republican power in the US Congress may well modify this policy. Already there are signs of a revival in funding for the Space Defence Initiative (SDI) which indicates a form of isolationism and would presumably require the removal of funding from the kind of international initiative described above. This appears to be a possibility despite the fact that it is not clear exactly where a nuclear missile threat to North America might come from in the new world order.

Another probably more durable arm to this policy is the development of a new strategic initiative for Asia. As mentioned in chapter 4, the first two of a projected series of Asia–Pacific Economic Co-operation summits were held in Seattle in November 1993 and in Jakarta in November 1994. They involved the governments of, in clockwise order around the Pacific: Australia, Indonesia, the Philippines, Thailand, Taiwan, China, South Korea, Japan, Canada and the USA. Notwithstanding the USA's existing commitment to NATO, the military implications of this cannot be entirely ignored. The USA might well be foreseeing, at least as one of its options, the Pacific replacing the Atlantic as the focus for global politico-economic power. This may signify in effect the end of the era of Western civilization as we have known it and the beginnings of a new global phase with its core partially in post-Confucian culture. Meanwhile the idea of economic co-operation around the Pacific Rim already exists and provision for military stability is a necessary adjunct to this at least. It is particularly so since considerable swathes of Asia, for instance India and eastern Russia, do not appear in the scenario at all. Earlier, in 1991, the Japanese government publicly declared 'the Kaifu doctrine', a vision of an Asian economic area with Japan as its superpower. Clearly the USA does not want to be excluded from this broad idea and thereby possibly totally eclipsed by Japan's politico-economic power in the twenty-first century.

In Europe the trend towards global military alliances progresses too. In October 1994 the British government announced that it was earmarking forces for a more integrated European command arrangement. The putative European pillar of NATO, the Western European Union, was originally formed in the early Cold War days of 1955 and at the time of writing is expected to be incorporated into the European Union. This will involve some shifting of France's previous boycott of NATO. The precise role proposed for a revived WEU is similar to that envisaged for the US/UN forces described above, that is humanitarian intercession, peacemaking and peacekeeping. The broad outcome of these changes would involve the USA, still the most powerful nation-state militarily, being linked both through NATO with Europe and through a Pacific–Asia treaty with East Asia. All of this would be geared towards global peacekeeping. With the eastern European states demanding entry to NATO, this could leave Russia and some of the other former Soviet Union states in a dangerously isolated position, though the former Warsaw Pact countries joined the NATO powers in a North Atlantic Co-operation Council, in 1991 (see table 11). In addition to all of this, there is the volatile and uncoordinated concentration of Islamic states in the Middle East sitting astride the greater part of the world's energy resources with double the global average of its population permanently under arms. The world order has become a global system in terms of both the universalization of modern industrially produced armaments and the existence of military alliances designed for global 'policing'. The kind of balance of power which was held firmly in place for more than forty years by the Cold War is, however, unlikely to be replaced when even the USA wants to share the burden of its superpower status with a variety of organizations – the United Nations, NATO and whatever arrangement is made between the Pacific–Asian states. The implications of this are not clear. In the

Table 11 *Membership of the North Atlantic Treaty Organization (NATO) and the North Atlantic Co-operation Council (NACC) as at October 1994*

Date of joining	
1949	*North Atlantic Treaty Organization* formed to include Belgium, Canada, Denmark, France, Iceland, Italy, Luxembourg, Netherlands, Norway, Portugal, UK, and USA
1952	Greece, Turkey
1955	German Federal Republic (West Germany)
1966	France withdraws its forces from NATO command but remains a member of the alliance
1982	Spain
1991	*North Atlantic Co-operation Council* formed to include NATO members and former Warsaw Pact countries: Albania, Armenia, Azerbaijan, Belarus, Bulgaria, Czech Republic, Estonia, Georgia, Hungary, Kazakhstan, Kirghizia, Latvia, Lithuania, Moldova, Poland, Romania, Russia, Slovakia, Tajikistan, Turkmenistan, Ukraine, Uzbekistan (Finland has observer status)

nineteenth century, when Britain was the world's superpower, elements of culture were absorbed with the power relationship of the Pax Britannica. People all over the world were made to recognize what was British and had a clear idea of Britishness, even if there were ways in which it proved to be a false impression. Subsequently, during the twentieth century, the Americanization of the world in cultural terms has been associated with what has sometimes been referred to as the Pax Americana. Global culture is extremely pervasive but it is not detachable from hegemonic politico-economic power. Possibly this is the beginning of a truly global political order based on a series of interlocking military alliances and supported by interdependent global production and division of labour. What might disrupt this are the global religions and a revival of Judaeo/Christian– Islamic conflict. Given the diaspora of both religions it would be a messy affair not necessarily restricted to the Middle East but resembling something like the tragedy of the former Yugoslavia. In fact, it would be something to tax severely the peacekeeping capabilities of revitalized forms of the United Nations and NATO.

7 Global Social Movements

Zsuzsa Hegedüs suggests that the 1980s witnessed 'a massive and unexpected emergence of new movements on a global scale' and, furthermore, that 'these new movements are usually not even integrated in the field of "new" social movements' (1990: 263–4). She sees the 1980s movements as being of a different order from, but building upon, the collective movements of the 1970s in peace, feminism and environmentalism. Above all she sees them creating a new awareness of personal responsibility for the collective future in all of its dimensions. Where the 1970s movements were collective confrontations with the orthodox consensus, those of the 1980s focused much more on the individual and the individual's approach to society through the cycle of their everyday lives. This is a good illustration of what Ulrich Beck (1988, 1992) has termed 'the reflexivity of modernity', using the environmentalist movement as a prime example. The concept is also used by Anthony Giddens (1990: 36–45, 1991) and Scott Lash (1993, 1994). Giddens couples this term with the notion of 'life politics' as the equivalent in late modernity of the emancipatory politics of the earlier stages of modernization. Furthermore, Beck (1994) sees the tendencies in social interaction referred to here as nothing less than 'the reinvention of politics' at a stage in social development at which risk – for instance the risk of nuclear destruction or irreversible environmental damage – has the appearance of being detached from and beyond the powers of all forms of social and political organization. Therefore individuals are constrained to take whatever action they can in terms of their own lives and, at the same time, they are further enabled in this by the new technological media of late modernity.

Hegedüs's approach is essentially optimistic, interpreting collective demonstrations of protest as transitional and as enabling the truly global nature of individualistic responses to be expressed, so that people think globally at whatever level they are engaging in social interaction. She stresses concepts of empowerment and self-determination in her arguments, emphasizing the widespread empowerment of the individual as a force for change potentially more effective than formal organization in a society which to all intents and purposes has become globalized. She concludes her arguments about the 'new' social movements with the statement that 'by their genuinely new manner of *individualising* planetary problems, they "*globalise*" individuals throughout the world, engendering a new way of thinking and acting; that is, a *new ethic of responsibility* and a *new practice of self-determination and solidarity*' (p. 277). The movements she uses by way of illustration had not achieved all their goals at the time that she was writing. They included Solidarity in Poland, a movement which combined with other similar movements and arguably produced the collapse of the Soviet-dominated eastern European regimes; the anti-apartheid movement in South Africa, since translated successfully into government; and 'people power' in the Philippines, which brought down the corrupt and repressive Marcos regime.

There is a clear implication that the change Hegedüs claims to have observed coincides with the revolution in global communication technology, although she does not go into this other than in a reference to the 'Live Aid' rock concert in aid of famine relief. This example did reach the largest media audience ever, however, estimated at almost one-third of the world's population. The 1980s was a time when, for instance, the cost of a basic television set was brought down to a level which even people in the less developed countries could afford. The cheap or communally used television set; personal and lap-top computers rather than mainframe data processing; and desktop publishing rather than printing presses – these are all varied examples of ways in which globalized institutions may be emancipatory in enabling people to do things that they could not do before. This is, I think, the essence of what Hegedüs is saying. Paul Ekins (1992) goes so far as to refer to the new environmental awareness as 'a new world order', somewhat confusingly given the phrase's military connotations. But there is a similar emphasis in his writing on an individual-istic approach to problems and the breaking of old patterns of behaviour. Certainly, many new forms of mass participation contrast in some important ways with the old. Wider access to share owner-ship, for example, has affected capitalism to some extent, but there remain serious problems of control, as small shareholders still have no power to influence company policies. For most people, contem-porary connections with capital remain indirect through insurance policies, pensions schemes and trades union funds. Significant partici-pation in mass consumption is, arguably, much more accessible and is surely available to everyone in some way or other. But there is still the problem of pricing and people can only consume in quantity to the level that they can afford. By contrast, mass communication coupled with the electronic revolution has, I would argue, progressed to another level of distribution whereby in effect, whatever one's socio-economic position, it can hardly be avoided.

John Boli and George M. Thomas (1990) propose the study of international non-government organizations (INGOs) as a means of analysing global social movements. As these writers define it, the category covers a wide range of organizations and, in their extensive compilation, 17.5 per cent of INGOs are in the natural sciences and a further 10 per cent in sport. Those addressing such issues as environ-mental concern and peace are 1970s movements in the sense em-ployed by Hegedüs. But Boli and Thomas go on to explore the ways in which individualism has nevertheless contributed to such organiza-tions, reversing Hegedüs's order in which collectivism gives way to increased individual awareness. They suggest that whatever consti-tutes world culture or world society is far from clear, but that its definition might be served by observing the ways in which global knowledge is transformed into global collective action, resulting in the formation of organizations on a global scale. There is certainly no such thing as a global polity in any integrated or formal hierarchical sense but there is undoubtedly a nation-state system. This has be-come more complex through the creation of more nation-states and as a consequence, they argue, the number of INGOs has increased in reaction to the complexity of relationships and counter-relationships between states. Their tentative inference from this, which connects with Hegedüs's thesis, is that it is the individualism in world culture which has produced the capacity for such a plethora of INGOs. The turning away to some extent from the formal authority invested in the nation-state is directed towards forms of non-governmental organization. This is coupled with the enabling effects of new communication technologies.

Furthermore, they assert, 'strong' national cultures such as French culture are implicated in global culture by their centrality to the politics of the nation-state system, while 'weaker' ones, such as Filipino culture, are implicated by their greater integration into global culture. This concept of a duality of national connections with world society is, I think, an interesting one because it allows for the power differentials which undoubtedly exist between nation-states, while stressing different dimensions to cultural integration. Thus, we might infer that the part played by France in the global environmental movement is as much a function of its government's aggressive stance towards Greenpeace as it is of popular support for the movement amongst the French people. Similarly, the Filipino government's indifference to environmental concerns does not prevent Filipinos from becoming involved through their exposure and susceptibility to global mass communications. This latter effect is enhanced because, like other peoples in less developed countries, the Filipinos are consumers rather than producers of the global media.

The peace movement and the feminist movement

Artur Meier (1990) takes up the case of the peace movement and, like Hegedüs, makes special reference to 1980s developments, stressing a broad popular base which he claims it did not have before. His implication is that, as a global movement, its contributions from the 1980s onwards have come from all social strata: from large and small groups distributed about the world; from other movements like feminism; from east and west of the old Cold War divide; and even from the heads of some nation-states. The peace movement is, of course, more directly political than some other movements. It has a clear adversary in the shape of the military–industrial complex and its apparently uncontrolled creation of the power to destroy all other aspects of civilization and even human life itself. Meier emphasizes that reaction to this has produced a movement that is 'really global in its existence' and 'significantly non-class based' (p. 257). Coupled with this is the argument that the movement was strengthened by the entry of many people from the professions or who were preparing for professional careers, particularly in the public sector, who during the 1980s experienced an erosion of their perceived privileges and rewards. If it is accepted that they attributed their losses largely to the burden of the arms race then Meier appears to be putting together an argument for at least the partial success of the movement, given the events of 1989 and what has been seen since then as a process of demilitarization (Shaw 1991). Certainly in terms of political rhetoric the so-called 'peace dividend' has been largely directed at the redistribution of considerable amounts of former arms spending. Although there is not much evidence that it has been directed significantly at public sector employment, Meier nevertheless appears convinced that 'the movement against the armament complex is obviously linked with the struggle for social progress' (p. 260).

Jan Aart Scholte (1993: 33) touches on the dimensions of the peace movement when he tries to clarify the term 'world perspective'. He argues that the words 'international' and 'world' are not interchangeable in this context. In particular he argues that 'To maintain that social relations have an important international dimension is not to hold that the international constitutes the motor of social change.' Here he is referring to the precise way in which, for example, the Greenham Common women's peace camp was a means of advancing a world perspective which opposed the existing world order and the liberal norms of society. A local, or at most a national, action in itself, it reached out to similar actions elsewhere and contributed to a world perspective and to world movements, in this case both the peace movement and the feminist movement. This was achieved independently of formal organization and in direct confrontation with the power of international alliances, in fact flying in the face of the accepted norms of liberal-democratic society. It could not be seen as part of existing international dimensions, although it achieved an international impact, but it may well be seen as part of the 'motor of social change', to use Scholte's term. Social change is not guaranteed by international relationships but it may well be influenced by a perspective that is truly global, a 'world perspective' in Scholte's terms. In this sense the actions of the women at Greenham Common may be distinguished from comparable previous actions. These actions were globalized through the women's movement and the peace movement, but each in what Hegedüs sees as their 1980s forms, mobilizing the individual conscience through global awareness or a 'world perspective'.

Scholte goes on to develop this premise in the language of world-system theory which, with its economistic leaning, I do not consider that fruitful a path to take. More helpful is his assertion that 'World ecology braids together international, national and local environmental issues, where none is reducible to the others' (p. 33). This is a point also taken up by Princen et al. (1994). Above all, Scholte's conclusion that contacts between strangers are a powerful driving force for social change is one that is clearly of great relevance to the analysis of globalization. Peterson and Runyan (1993: 126) also take this up in connection with the women's peace encampments, pointing out that during the 1980s these arose at Greenham Common and Molesworth in England, Comiso in Italy, Hunsrück in West Germany, Seneca and Puget Sound in the United States, Nanoose in Canada, Soesterburg in Holland, and Pine Gap in Australia. Peterson and Runyan's main point is the now familiar one taken from the writings of Virginia Woolf: 'As a woman I have no country . . . my country is the whole world.'

In the examples cited here, there is the common factor of global awareness and the creation of a world perspective in the pursuit of peace. The world order, referred to here in the sense of the global military order, was maintained by the governments of the superpowers with a policy of mutually assured destruction through the threatened use of nuclear weapons. This was the basis for a balance of power. It pertained right through the period of the Cold War, but competition in nuclear weapons systems was intensified during the 1980s when the US Reagan administration sought to achieve clear superiority by means of its extremely ambitious Space Defence Initiative (SDI), better known as the 'Star Wars Programme'. As the writers discussed above have observed, this was also the decade when global protest movements tended to take on a new form, not one of action through existing organizations linked internationally, but one of individual consciousness linked through global awareness. That these things happened at the same time was in fact no coincidence, because it was in this decade that the effects of the electronic revolution were generally intensified. As well as advancing the possibilities for weapons systems the 1980s produced more pervasive communications media that were not only enabling but also more freely available. The television set had long become a standard item of furniture in the home for virtually everyone in the West and access to TV was available one way or another for many people in the less developed countries too. But during the 1980s this compelling medium of communication was enhanced by the more or less instantaneous global diffusion of imagery through the use of satellite technology. With the technology developed into portable forms even the women in the peace camps could watch the progress of the renewed arms race of the 1980s and reactions to it. Where they lacked direct access they could derive the information from their considerable support networks. Amongst other things electronic technology has presented tremendous capacities to extend the outcome of social interaction through time and space in the mobilization of individual consciences.

The environmental movement

In pre-industrial societies most people lived in a rural setting with a cycle of activities which Émile Durkheim described in terms of mechanical social solidarity and division of labour. This brought them routinely into direct contact with the natural environment and that environment was the local one. They had little idea of its global implications but they were environmentally friendly, in today's jargon, by comparison with the mass consumers of an industrialized and urbanized modern society. Their agrarian activities did little to damage the global environment.

So the story goes in the conventional explanation for contemporary environmental problems and the essential difference between traditional and modern society. But in fact we are now learning from late modern scientific techniques that the industrial activity which existed on the margins of majority agricultural activity in the past can be detected through its impact on the global environment. Ice core readings from the Antarctic have yielded evidence, for instance, of the Roman lead industry at its height when output was at a level not exceeded by any metal production until the eighteenth-century onset of the Industrial Revolution (Siegenthaler and Oeschger 1987). In this, of course, we in late modernity are backtracking in order to understand better our present predicament. Amongst the things that worry us are problems of global warming and rising sea-levels with the melting of the ice-caps; the depletion of the ozone layer and its implications for the incidence of human skin cancer; the deterioration of air quality due to carbon monoxide emission from the widespread use of motor vehicles; and so on. Obviously there are special trouble spots in each of these cases, but intrinsically they have one thing in common: they are universal problems threatening everyone – the human race and the planet on which it lives. If the emissions of the Roman lead industry can be detected in the Antarctic ice what are the effects of an integrated global economy operating with mass production through a globalized division of labour and, in effect, global production lines? Clearly we are all consumers, most especially those of us in the West, and in order to produce an effective remedy for environmental damage our patterns of living have to change significantly. In the often-repeated warning of Jonathon Porritt (1988: 20), 'we must be prepared to reduce our own standard of living'. However, there can be little doubt that, without consensus and careful planning, this would undermine the global economy and thereby threaten the nation-state system and the world order, the bases for global political stability.

At this point it is perhaps worth remembering that not all the changes wrought upon the environment are due to industrial activities. During the various phases of European colonialism there were many botanical transfers between the continents and regions of the world which caused transformations in the balance of the natural environment. Most people have heard of the ill-fated voyage of the British naval vessel the *Bounty* in 1789, but few are familiar with its intended purpose. It was to transplant the 'breadfruit' of the tree *Artocarpus incisa* from the South Pacific to the West Indies because of its potential to feed slaves on colonial plantations. There were, in fact, many such transfers of plants from one environment to another. The former British colony of the Gold Coast (now of course independent and known as Ghana) is typical of several territories on the west coast of Africa that had much of their cultivable land area turned over to the cultivation of the cocoa bean. Similarly the Malaysian archipelago and other parts of the world were utilized for rubber plantations when the demand for that commodity increased at the beginning of the twentieth century. As with cocoa, the rubber plant occurs naturally in Latin America. A more dramatic example of environmental change, however, followed the introduction of honey bees into New Zealand from England in 1839 after European plants and animals had already been taken there. Until that time there had been no effective insect pollinators on the islands and the flora were pollinated by other means such as birds, through their feeding, or simply by the carrying of pollen on the wind. The new introductions worked symbiotically with plants (e.g. cereals and fruit trees) and animals (e.g. sheep, horses and cattle) to facilitate the rapid spread of European flora at the expense of naturally occurring plants. There are also examples of naturally occurring botanical transfers of course, but these examples show how the artificial transmission of crops between the continents can bring about relatively rapid and very extensive changes. The global culture has therefore had a global influence at the natural as well as the social level and during the twentieth century there have been some intentional and co-ordinated changes to the natural environment planned on a global scale. The so-called 'Green Revolution' in cereals production is a prime example. It involved the intentional disruption of traditional patterns of agriculture and the use of capital-intensive fertilizers and machinery with the entirely laudable goal of increasing outputs of basic food-stuffs in areas of poverty endemically threatened with famine. Unfortunately the environmental changes were not accompanied by the necessary social changes which would have ensured that the benefits reached the mass of people for whom they were intended.

The environmental movement was from its beginnings directed at global problems and it has therefore tended to operate on a global level, notwithstanding the importance of local groups. 'Think globally, act locally' has been the slogan, but Kate Burningham and Martin O'Brien (1994) counsel us to consider the political dimension and the variety of possibilities for the definition of environment and environmentalism. For instance, there are many ways in which the movement has benefited from the electronic media of communication and their capacity to be used to mobilize individual consciences. In the early 1970s the Club of Rome's 'Limits to Growth' set out the implications of continuous economic growth, while the *Blueprint for Survival* acted as a kind of manifesto for organizations like Friends of the Earth. Organizations of this type came to make up the formally organized part of the green movement, but it is more recently, during the 1980s, that a wider range of individuals has been drawn into environmental activity, sometimes through small local groups working at grassroots level. Supermarket chains now feel they should include 'environmentally friendly' products in their ranges, for example, and local councils organize collection points for the recycling of glass containers, paper and metal cans. During this same decade, Greenpeace developed the reputation of being a more radical organization, prepared to engage in direct confrontation with environmental offenders and even to break the law. However, although this would appear to be the impression of the majority of people, not everyone agrees with it. Steven Yearley (1994: 156), for example, argues that, of the environmental lobby in Britain, 'the groups which are both radical and effective tend to be centralized'. He takes up the view of a campaigning journalist who has asserted that, 'From a small grouping at the beginning of the eighties, Greenpeace displays all the trappings of a multi-national company or a civil service department' (Allen 1992: 23). It can hardly be denied that, in order to pursue its environmental concerns around the world, Greenpeace has developed into a form of transnational organization comparable in principle and in the global extent of its activities to some of the companies which it opposes. It draws expertise from different nation-states and deploys technology according to its strategic plans. It has learned to lobby governments and to mobilize public support taking advantage of the global media and the raised consciousness of a global movement. Leslie Sklair describes this type of organization as a 'transnational environmentalist organization' (TEO). He approaches his definition thus, expanding on the connections, as he sees them, between transnational corporations and transnational environmentalist organizations:

One way to attack this problem is to draw out the relationships between the characteristics of global capitalism, the TNCs, and those of the global environmentalist system, the trans-national environmentalist organizations (TEOs). These relationships straddle the spectrum from direct and indirect TNC sponsorship and support of TEOs to downright hostility and occasional violence between the parties and their allies. A first approximation of TEOs would certainly include the United Nations Environmental Programme, the World Conservation Union (formerly International Union for the Conservation of Nature), Worldwide Fund for Nature, Friends of the Earth, Greenpeace and the International Organization of Consumers Unions. To this list must be added the myriad of global environmentalist organizations that mushroomed around the Bruntland Report and the 1992 UN Conference on Environment and Development in Rio de Janeiro and its aftermath. (Sklair 1994: 210)

The transnational form of some environmental organizations should not be unexpected given the dimensions of their remit: the planet and the life upon it. This is precisely the same dimension in which the transnational corporations operate. As suggested in an earlier chapter, put simply the TNCs range the world in search of favourably priced raw materials and labour for production, and their finished manufactures too must be marketed globally for the maximum potential return on investment. Therefore, networks of supply, manufacture and marketing are assembled to satisfy the demands of mass consumption. Put equally simply, part of the reason why transnational environmentalist organizations exist is that some of the ways in which the TNCs go about their global activities are regarded as damaging to the environment.

Scott Lash and John Urry (1994: 292) point out that in modernity, until fairly recently, 'it was a characteristic of organized capitalism that a whole range of economic and social problems was thought to be soluble at the level of the nation-state', but now, in late modernity (or post-modernity in their terms), 'disorganized capitalism disorganizes such a national strategy'. Late modernity is the period when society's problems can no longer be solved at the national level because in so many ways society is no longer a national society but a global or world society. Nevertheless there remains interpenetration between the global and the local and, as I have argued, it is through this that global institutions are reproduced. The reactions of human beings to environmental damage are reproduced and institutionalized through this process as much as the economic actions which are seen to cause it. Globalization in the environmental movement is not only – in fact it is not mainly – the activities of Greenpeace, although these may be the ones reported in the global media. Rather, it is the global awareness reproduced through the interpenetration of universalistic influences derived from transnational networks and particularistic reproductions of these influences at the local level. As Lash and Urry (p. 298) put it, global awareness of environmentalism has been potentiated by the 'global mass media which have generated an "imagined community" of all societies inhabiting "one earth" (cf. Friends of *the* Earth)'. Both Friends of the Earth, with its survivalist approach, and Greenpeace, with its vigorous protectionist actions, have been mentioned here, but there is another significant thread to the way in which the environmentalist thinking has been developed. This is the Gaia hypothesis, the concept that the Earth is a superordinate organism and has to be respected as such. There is a mystical side to this – the name 'Gaia' means earth goddess – but the principle that, for instance, the atmosphere is a system of equilibrium involving levels of gaseous content linked to levels of temperature, is clearly of relevance to any form of environmentalism. In this perspective a naturally occurring phenomenon, even on the scale of the Amazon basin's tropical rainforest, should be treated with as much respect as any living organism. The 'oneness' of the Earth, the life upon it and most especially the human race's responsibilities in this are accentuated. The problem then becomes clear. Human beings have powers distinct from the rest of the environment and they have developed these powers over some thousands of years in order to provide themselves with better standards of living. In generic terms, production is the process of extraction from the environment, processing and distribution. The development of this activity to truly global proportions marks the point at which production for human provision can clearly be seen to come into conflict with the environment as a whole – Earth, life and people.

The 'oneness' of Earth, life and people can be seen in yet another context. The creation of global awareness has given rise to what Peter Beyer (1994: 206) describes as an 'upsurge' of religious environmentalism. As he points out, when the 307-member World Council of Churches met in Seoul in 1990, it was under the rubric of 'Justice, Peace and the Integrity of Creation'. To this he adds the corollary that when the World Wildlife Federation held its twenty-fifth anniversary meeting it chose to do so in Assisi, the birthplace of St Francis (p. 209). Beyer puts the environmental issue in context with other global issues thus: 'the degree to which Third World underdevelopment is a product of First World development may be a matter for debate; the radioactive fallout in Britain, Scandinavia, and elsewhere as a result of the Chernobyl disaster far less so' (p. 208). Here, there is a sense again in which the universals of global environmental damage and global awareness of it are reproduced in a variety of particularistic settings which involve individual human beings across the whole range of their activities, including, as in this example, religious allegiance. In religious environmentalism, Beyer (pp. 217–18) distinguishes between 'eco-spirituality', in which there is an emphasis on the integrity of creation; 'eco-justice', in which principles of participation and sustainability are combined; and 'eco-traditionalism', in which there is determination to achieve environmentalist objectives through established religious principles. These are clearly Christian-oriented categories, and we should perhaps not lose sight of Max Weber's classification of the world religions which includes Confucianism, Hinduism, Buddhism and Islam as well as Christianity because of the influence of each across cultural and political boundaries. In a recent work devoted to the place of Islam in the contemporary globalized society, Bryan S. Turner (1994: 105) suggests that 'Different world religions have obviously had different conceptions of the nature of the world, and our contemporary view of the globe can be seen as partly shaped by these "primitive" attempts to think globally.' In the late modern world these religions not only transcend nation-state borders but also cut across the economic core regions, the 'triad' of North America, Europe and East Asia, in the terminology used in chapter 4. World religions, then, form another dimension to globalizing influences in the multiplicity of conjunctions between the global and the local that form the notion of world society.

In any overarching theory of environmentalism, the fundamental principle must be that the individual stands in some kind of relationship with the environment. In tribal society it is easy to see that this relationship is straightforward. The complications come with civilization. As city life became physically separated from rural life, city dwellers became detached from a day-to-day, cycle-of-the-seasons relationship with the environment. With the onset of modernity the twin transformations of industrialization and urbanization began to penetrate the whole of society causing, so to speak, the urban mode to spill out into the rural. The majority of the population became urbanized and rural agriculture became industrialized as part of the universalizing effect. From the time that this truly took hold, the whole of society has effectively existed in a created environment and the direct relationship between social life and the natural environment has to all intents and purposes been lost completely. The transformation of modernity completed civilization's intercession in the relationship between the individual and the environment. Subsequently, the individual has been socialized in a world in which global systems and global knowledge are increasingly taken for granted but in which a direct relationship with the environment no longer exists at all. The task which the environmentalist movement has taken on is to attempt to redress the balance. In early modernity people thought that technology could solve all of society's problems. In late modernity the younger generation knows nothing but fast-changing electronic technology which makes anything seem possible in a rather different way. Taking the optimistic view, where the breakthrough of mechanical technology was the delivery of goods, that of electronic power is in the delivery of knowledge. The interpenetration of the local and the global may therefore be a means of recreating tribal society's awareness of the environment and applying this to late modernity's post-Fordist global production techniques.

Conclusion
The Individual and the Global

The single most important factor in globalization is that the global enters into our local day-to-day reproduction of social institutions. In late modernity, throughout the individual's life-cycle he or she is socialized in the light of global knowledge, global awareness and global imagery. As Anthony Giddens puts it, traditional institutions are 'disembedded', to be replaced by those derived from globalized communication, authorization, allocation and sanction.

Even face-to-face communication and mass communications confined within the nation-state become imbued with global significa-tion. In chapter 5 I outlined how developing technologies have accelerated the production and exchange of information on a global scale. The individual now communicates against the background of a huge range of potential mass communication channels.

National politics have become imbued with global politics, since the nation-state is part of the global nation-state system. I argued in chapter 3 that the citizen of a nation-state now faces a number of sources of apparent authority ranging from the sub-national to the supra-national, but also including the non-governmental.

Local and national economies have only very limited indepen-dence because they form parts of the interdependent global economy. As shown in chapter 4, the global economy has produced shifting networks of interdependence and the focal points of econ-omic exchange have changed. It is on this basis that individual human beings struggle to maintain their connection with production and consumption, in the generic sense of the individual–environment subsistence relationship.

Group sanction is still a powerful social institution amongst people who know each other, but otherwise the legitimation of actions is through formal codes, the prime example of which is the legal system. In this sphere the nation-state retains most of its legal jurisdiction, but law enforcement is increasingly beset by globalized criminal activities, in some cases described as terrorism, and there are calls for international responses. In this respect law enforcement shades off into military activity and in the last resort global sanctions are enforced by full-scale military activity. Chapter 6 described how the world order, held in place for almost forty-five years by the strategic imperatives of the Cold War, was reduced to a state of flux by the collapse of the Soviet Union. In this respect, the individual's fortunes as a civilian, soldier, or refugee depend upon their relative position in terms of the world order.

In all of these examples of developments in social institutions we must take account of the twin dimensions of time and space. The individual stands in relationship to the global at specific points in time and space, but the process of globalization has increasingly linked these points through the global institutions of communication, polity, economy and sanction. In his most recent work Giddens (1994) refers to this as 'post-traditional society'. The certainties of traditional society are removed as traditional institutions give way to the globalization of culture. Like all acts of social reproduction the process is a reflexive one, but reflection in modernity involves reference to different kinds of authority. In traditional society, tradition itself is the form of authority received through figures imbued with combinations of mystical and theological power. In post-traditional society authority is vested in trained 'experts' whose power lies in rational forms of knowledge, distanced through time and space as part of the globalized culture. Tradition is thereby replaced by routine as the main form of integration for society and the greater part of social activity takes place on the basis of trust – the trust of the individual in the expertise of a range of specialists most of whom he or she will never meet. Trust, for instance, that electricity will be constantly forthcoming to power the range of artefacts on which day-to-day life depends – trust that somewhere, someone will be ensuring that the nuclear reactors will not be going into meltdown – trust in the experts who say that we should use less energy in order to lessen the risks associated with global warming – trust in the specialists who tell us to eat less fat and give up smoking in order to avoid the killer diseases of late modernity.

Scott Lash and John Urry (1994: 38) argue that Giddens's notion of reflexivity 'mainly functions to reproduce structures', whereas it is Ulrich Beck's version that 'leads mainly to the critical change of social structures'. They have interpreted Giddens's (1990, 1991, 1992) approach as concentrated upon the self-reflexivity of the individual and Beck's (1992) comparable work on modernity as directed more effectively at the norms and structures of society. This appears to be a common interpretation of Giddens's work (cf. Robertson 1992: 144–5) and yet the self-reflexivity of the individual on which it is centred is directed at a systematic questioning of the 'expert systems' referred to above. Lash and Urry seem to recognize this themselves (1994: 39), despite their criticism. In fact, both Beck and Giddens seem agreed on the place of risk in late modern society and on the growing refusal of people to accept expert assurances about its dangers. If, in the nineteenth century, those people who understood it and had access to its benefits rejoiced in the bounty of modernity and its scientific–technological wonders, the people of late modernity are cultured to expect mass consumption but are increasingly sufficiently well informed to develop doubts about its benefits. This *is* self-reflexivity and it is stimulated by negative experiences shared on a global scale, like for instance the Chernobyl disaster. It is individualism, enabled by mass education and encouraged by post-1960s permissiveness and self-awareness.

Lash and Urry (1994: 74–5) describe Japanese post-Fordist manufacturing as a form of 'collective reflexivity'. They are mainly referring to the use of quality circles and other forms of horizontal collective responsibility in Japanese and East Asian manufacturing industry and to the *kanban* approach to production scheduling. But there is another side to this. Post-Fordist production systems offer the customer more flexible product ranges and encourage the idea of individualism in consumption. Post-Fordist consumption is still mass consumption but consumer reflexivity is encouraged. Fordism's insistence that the customer should accept what the producer offers is replaced in post-Fordism by the principle that customers can, if not design, at least specify the configuration of the product. More importantly, *kanban* production scheduling can accommodate this and still operate on lower stockholdings and therefore less capital investment.

Reflexivity might well appear to be a quality running right through the social organization of late modernity, from the individual to the global. In Lash and Urry (1994: 306), however, there is the suggestion that post-Fordism might be taken as the end of mass production. This is, I think, mistaken. Rather, post-Fordism is a different way of doing mass production. The quantities produced are the same, but better production planning enables the output to be more varied. Lash and Urry are also doubtful about the concept of a global culture and seem to prefer the notion of 'a number of processes which are producing the globalization of culture' (p. 306). One illustration they use is that of Arjun Appadurai's (1990) five dimensions to global cultural flow – ethnoscapes, technoscapes, finanscapes, mediascapes, ideoscapes – which were described in chapter 5. These writers confirm Roland Robertson's argument that such influences are of a different order from relationships between nation-states. Equally, they accept that the effects of the globalization of culture are different from those of a dominant ideology (cf. Parkin 1971; Abercrombie et al. 1980, 1990). I should have thought that there is no problem with the concept of a global culture which has a number of dimensions to it, and in this book I have preferred to see the cultural aspects of globalization in terms of such dimensions.

From Roland Robertson's (1992: 182) work I should want to take the proposition that globalization is basically a contested process. His emphasis on the interpenetration of universalistic influences and particularistic reactions is, I believe, the clearest conceptualization of the way in which the globalization process was begun by Western dominance but is now quite definitely something different. Using Giddens's principle of the 'duality of structure', flows of global culture in time and space cannot exist unless they are reproduced at points of human contact in passing moments of time. Such reproduction can never be entirely a passive process. In the active reproduction of global culture, that which we might recognize as social change largely occurs in the form of Robertson's interpenetration of the universal and the particular. The outcome in late modernity is that the reproduction of global cultural flows has been subjected to a number of particularistic influences and the West certainly does not control the process any longer. The best example of this is Japanese and East Asian manufacturing success and the contribution to this of particular cultural influences, principally consisting of Confucian (or post-Confucian) socialization processes and institutionalized forms of social group. These have been significant in the development of organizational innovations. What Robertson neglects in his treatment of these developments is that reactions to globalization are themselves articulated through global institutions. Once a global framework has been constructed it is by definition difficult to avoid. Yet he seems to be arguing that differentiation or even 'de-differentiation' (1992: 144) can still take place independently of global cultural flows. To take his example of fundamentalism, the post-1979 establishment of a Twelver Shi'a Islamic Republic in Iran was organized by making all the institutional tiers of a modern nation-state – including central and local government, courts and judicial system – subject to the principles of Shi'a Islamic theology. In other words, contemporary Iran contains the universal institutions of the nation-state but they have been reproduced in the particular form of Shi'a Islamic prescription. There are many obvious examples of this. When British colonialists claimed to have discovered Victoria Falls what they were really saying was that they had added it to the pool of global knowledge. When Africans reaffirm their obvious prior knowledge of the falls they do so as a conscious reaction to colonial arrogance which was a global and globalizing influence in the nineteenth and early twentieth centuries. In this way the Africanness of the Victoria Falls is asserted, whereas without colonialism it would have simply been taken for granted. Ironically, they remain known as the Victoria Falls.

Robertson also seems determined to keep separate modernization and globalization (1992: 170). Yet the proposition that modernity led to globalization seems to me unexceptional. Surely it was the 'Enlightenment project' and the notion of the 'standard of civilization' that provided the justification for the encouraged and sometimes enforced global spread of European institutions? These are hallmarks of modernity – at least of early modernity. Certainly there are elements of globalizing influences before modernity but they could hardly have developed into a full global culture without advances in travel and communication, the nation-state system, the global economy, and so on. In the modern era many more people have held accurate and informed impressions of the world in their heads than could have been the case before. Social institutions are reproduced with global awareness or even in global terms as a result. Robertson talks about people being 'condemned to modernity'; surely by the same token they are condemned to globalization? Once global awareness is achieved how is it possible to act independently of it? Even reactions to the influences of global cultural flows are enacted with global awareness. In fact, Robertson goes on to affirm that 'locality is, to put it simply, globally institutionalized' (p. 172) – and, with reference to hard-nosed commercial instrumentality, that the Japanese word 'glocalize' and its employment as a marketing buzzword must be recognized amongst 'directly "real world" attempts to bring the global . . . into conjunction with the local' (pp. 173–4). Indeed, I think that the most fruitful part of Robertson's work is his development of Immanuel Wallerstein's simple concept of 'universalism through particularism, and particularism through universalism' (1984: 166–7). Appadurai (1990: 17) describes the same conjunction in terms of the twin Enlightenment ideas of 'the triumphantly universal and the resiliently particular'. For Robertson it becomes a central concept:

> My own argument involves the attempt to preserve direct attention *both* to particularity and difference *and* to universality and homogeneity. It rests largely on the thesis that we are, in the late twentieth century, witnesses to – and participants in – a massive, twofold process involving *the interpenetration of the universalization of particularism and the particularization of universalism* . . . (1992: 100)

In these terms post-Fordist manufacturing has been interpreted very effectively as the connection of 'globewide universalistic supply' with 'particularistic demand' through the further interpenetration of culture and economy. Here Robertson is articulating the conclusion of many researchers that social change cannot be explained by one overarching grand theory. Rather, he sees it as the result of interplay between not only the global and the local but also the various institutional dimensions that can be attributed to each. This has been expressed elsewhere in different ways. For instance, although he is generally sceptical about globalization, Anthony D. Smith shows that his scepticism may be attributable to the interpenetration of the universal and the particular:

> This is not to deny the global diffusion of some aspects of modern Euro-American culture, especially popular music, films, video, dress and some foods. The worldwide spread of consumer commodities, of art styles in furnishing, of architecture and the visual arts, not to mention the mass media and tourism, is evidence of a global nexus of markets for

similar products and the ability of consumer industries to mould shared tastes, in some degree at least. But even here, ethnic and class factors intrude. The appreciation and assimilation of Western styles and cultural products is generally adaptive: the audiences in Third World countries tend to interpret these products and experiences in ways that are specific to the perceptions and understanding of their own peoples. (1992: 66)

Jan Aart Scholte (1993: 10–11) draws attention to the situation whereby 'in the light of globalization and the transnational spread of many social transformations, a number of researchers across the spectrum of academic disciplines have in recent decades rejected endogenous models of history and have sought instead to explain social change in world perspective'. In particular he draws attention to Michael Mann's (1986: 503) conclusion from his wide-ranging study of the history of power that 'the sources of change are geographically and socially "promiscuous" – they do not all emanate from within the social and territorial space of the given "society".' Janet Abu-Lughod (1991: 132–3) projects some colourful illustrations of this. On the one hand, she describes the marketing in Tunis of familiar Western brands in the souk, while nearby artisans put the finishing touches to hand-sewn Gucci purses. On the other hand, in Europe and the USA there are cases of the popularization of mixed Western and oriental music produced by, in her example, a young male Bedouin rock-singer. These examples are significant because they bring out the relationship between the global and local for a range of differently placed individuals. Abu-Lughod (p. 134) distinguishes these modern examples from the pre-modern by reference to the term *univers cloisonné*, from the French historian Pierre Chaunu. This encapsulates perfectly a sense of the 'cultural condition' of traditional society which, for all but the elite few of its members, was a segmented and compartmentalized existence.

In terms of the relationship between the individual and the global, Robertson (1992: 59) regards the individual as one of four 'reference points' for the study of globalization. The other three are national society, the international system of societies, and the 'singular but not unified' conception of humankind. The individual seems to me to be the odd one out in this classification. The other three reference points are all social constructs. They form part of the overall social structure and they are created by the human individual. The individual reproduces the social structure, although sociologists and other observers of the process may analyse that structure through a number of dimensions. Critics of this viewpoint may argue that they are not constructs of the human individual in isolation but of the human individual as part of society. This cannot be denied but it is the human individual as a part of society who must hold these constructs in mind. A conception of the human individual and what it is to be one is also a mental construct, but it is the mental construct of a thinking human being and this must always be the starting-point. It is human beings who reproduce the institutions of society and, in that reproduction, there are the unacknowledged conditions of those institutions. In the Enlightenment project these have become those of the Enlightenment; in modernity, those of modernity; in the process of globalization, those of globalization. By the same token there are unintended consequences of the same order, that is in effect the extension in time and space of Enlightenment, modernity, globalization, etc.

Elsewhere, Robertson (1992: 114) refers, in connection with perestroika and glasnost in the former Soviet Union, to 'the problem of the relationship between societal identity, societal restructuring and participation in the globalization process'. This, he argues, reflects upon the openness of societies. It is therefore of great relevance to any study of globalization and especially to his principle of interpenetration between the universal and the particular. In broader terms this has been treated in a number of ways. For example, Friedrich Nietzsche's writing is an example of anti-Enlightenment, anti-universal thinking, while that of Jürgen Habermas may be taken to represent defence of the Enlightenment project. Jean François Lyotard's (1984) version of post-modernism purports to trace the movement of human faith away from 'engineered progress' – a discontinuity to modernity, while for Francis Fukuyama (1992), the collapse of the Soviet Union and what it stood for represents the 'end of history' and the final triumph of Western liberal-democratic capitalism as the true outcome of Enlightenment, modernity and globalization. There is a sense in which Robertson's principle of the interpenetration of the universal and the particular provides a concept which embraces all of these and that is why I think it is so important. This is especially so since it allows for the fact, which he emphasizes, that the outcome of the process remains 'up for grabs' (1992: 62). It is not at an end, *pace* Fukuyama, nor has it been substantially deflected in any particular direction, *pace* Nietzsche and Lyotard. The concept of global culture involves people in its reproduction of social institutions on a global scale. As a concept it can have practical meaning only in this sense, and the outcome is the continuous reproduction of global cultural flows. By this definition, therefore, global culture is subject to a continuous interplay between its universal aspects and those of its particularistic reproduction. In other words those who are subject to it are also involved in its reproduction and, as Robertson asserts, the global culture is therefore never crystallized but always 'up for grabs'.

Consider some random examples, plucked from consciousness and memory, of cultural reproduction upon a global scale:

A cosmopolitan set of 250 passengers on an Air France Boeing 747 jet airliner watches an 'in-flight movie'. It is a Franco-Russian film, *Urga*, set in Chinese Mongolia, in which a hard-drinking nomadic tribesman is showing everyone a picture which he claims is of his brother in America. It is, in fact, a picture of Sylvester Stallone originally intended for the promotion of an extremely violent film called *The Cobra*. A mile or so below, African villagers watch an episode of *Dynasty* in which the American ersatz aristocratic family suffer at the hands of a mythical and improbable central European dictatorship. They watch it on a black-and-white set manufactured by the Samsung Corporation in South Korea and during the commercial breaks are enjoined to keep up their consumption of Coca Cola. Elsewhere, across all five continents, a huge audience of television viewers watch, by satellite, Brazil beat Italy at football in the 1994 World Cup final in Los Angeles. In the outskirts of Rio da Janeiro, shanty-town dwellers are ecstatic that their national team are world champions again after many years of relative failure. In the morning some of them will be making a creditable attempt to recreate on the beach the sporting skills that they have seen. But for the moment they celebrate with salsa dance rhythms that have been *de rigueur* in discos throughout the world. In Angola, United Nations representatives are ensuring that an election conforms to Western standards when there are known risks of cheating and threats of violence against electors. In a provincial English town the turnout in a local by-election is so poor that the result means very little in terms of national politics. In urban centres around the world people are eating McDonald's hamburgers. The restaurants are staffed by local workers, mostly young, who seek to produce fast food to the standard McDonald's formula. In fact, there are some localized variations in the reproduction of the formula, both in the organization and in the food. At the McDonald's in Moscow and Beijing there are still long queues. Other people at a variety of locations are working on assembly lines manufacturing the components which come together at a few centralized points as the Ford Escort motor car. In Sri Lanka young women are sewing together fashion clothing recently designed in London. The garments they were working on two weeks ago are being purchased by other young women from chain stores in shopping malls across Europe. Outside Sarajevo, a Bosnian Serb sniper trains his AK-47 assault rifle on an exposed stretch of road where many civilians have been shot. In Somalia a US marine with an Armalite automatic rifle stands guard outside a food store, looking forward to his imminent return home.

Examples such as these to which one can instantly have recourse are an endless reminder of globalization.

Reactions to global cultural flows

In the academic world, Peterson and Runyan (1993: 29) make some interesting observations about the global reproduction of the study of international affairs when they question the preponderance of men in the field of international relations. They observe that the current state of the discipline was arrived at through a process by which 'Men checked with each other about what men were doing that was considered relevant to other men and was written by men primarily for male audiences!' They conclude that the reason for this is:

International relations distinguishes itself from political science generally by valuing matters of foreign policy over matters of domestic policy: relations between but not within states define its focus. Whereas domestic political observers and policy makers have had to grapple with voting behaviour, welfare state issues, domestic public interest groups,

and social movements – areas in which gender issues figure pro-
minently – IR practitioners have focused on national security (defined
most often in terms of military might), economic power (defined
typically by gross national product indicators), and international
organizations and regimes (made up of government and financial
elites). Not only are women infrequent actors in these matters of state,
but also IR orthodoxy sees no place for women in these high-stakes
games.

In another context, that of religion, concern about the reproduction
of particular social forms in the face of universalistic influences arises
and is expressed in a different way. Peter Beyer (1994) describes very
effectively the relationship between Muslims' fears about the
marginalization of their religion and the international publication of
Salman Rushdie's novel *The Satanic Verses*. As Beyer points out,
this novel is about the 'mutability of character under globalizing
conditions' but because the setting is the Islamic religion it caused a
furore.

> Many Muslims perceive it as an affront to what they hold most sacred
> and thereby a negation of themselves as actors in global society. The
> latter phrase is key. The Rushdie affair does more than demonstrate the
> link between religious faith and particularistic identity. On the whole,
> outraged Muslims are, in fact, not concerned that Rushdie's book will
> undermine their faith – all the less so since few devout Muslims will ever
> read it. What troubles them much more is the notion that they are being
> asked to surrender the core of that faith – the *immutable sacredness* of
> the Qur'an – as the price for full inclusion in a global system currently
> dominated by non-Muslims. Khomeini and many other Muslims equate
> the revitalization of Islam declared by *The Satanic Verses* with the
> marginalization of Muslims in the overall society. Khomeini's condem-
> nation of Rushdie is therefore part of a much larger Muslim effort to
> counter inequalities within the global system through the revitalization
> of Islamic particularity. (1994: 3)

I described earlier how the creation of a Twelver Shi'a Islamic Republic in Iran after the 1979 revolution in Iran which restored the
Ayatollah Khomeini to power involved the reproduction of the Western model of the nation-state with provision at all levels for the
safeguarding of Islamic ideals. It was not an attempt to block the
universalizing influence of globalization but to reproduce it within
particular institutional forms. With the Rushdie affair the process is

comparable. As Beyer further observes, 'The intent is to shape the global reality, not to negate it' (p. 3). The Muslim reaction to *The Satanic Verses* ensured that the book's sales were much greater than they would have been otherwise and that many more people attempted to read its difficult text. It is an example of the potential tension between universal and particular influences and it adds a further dimension to the concept of globalization. Islam itself is a global influence. There are large numbers of Muslims distributed about the world and large numbers of Christians. In the example of the Rushdie affair, the predominant Western form of globalization, which is universalistic but secular, came into collision with a particularistic theological form which also has global pretensions. It is in one sense a form of replay of the old antagonism between European Christianity and Middle Eastern Islam, but played out under contemporary conditions after a mostly secularized Western civilization has successfully formed the first truly global culture. Indeed it is from precisely the secular elements of Western civilization that the counter-reaction to Khomeini's *fatwa* came, although the Christian church was rather taken aback by such an extreme invocation of ecclesiastical law – the *shari'a*. In terms of Western culture and rationality it is, as Beyer observes, 'matters such as freedom of artistic expression and the sovereighty of states [that] are at the centre of the conflict, not religion' (p. 4). It can be expressed more forcefully than this. People in the West were outraged at the very idea that an Islamic cleric, however senior in the Iranian Shi'a hierarchy, could pronounce the death sentence upon a citizen of another nation-state. The effect is heightened by the fact that most Western states, with the exception of the USA, have abolished the death penalty. Additionally it came as a shock that a figure such as Khomeini – that is a Persian, not an Arab, and a minority Shi'a, not a Sunni Muslim – could have influence on such a scale, amongst Muslims generally. It is nowadays taken for granted that many influences will have a cross-border, inter-state effect. This is merely a part of the reproduction of global culture. But in the overwhelming majority of cases the influences are Western influences and the reaction to the prospect of Islamic culture having a similar effect provides evidence of selectivity in the acceptability, in Western eyes, of global influences. This example from Islam can be compared with reactions to the pronouncements of the so-called New Christian Right, or Christian fundamentalism as it is sometimes alternatively referred to, during the

1980s. Beyer (p. 112) interprets its pronouncements as reactions to what were seen as failures in American government policies. Internally, there had been the failure of the legacy of the New Deal – that is the particularly American application of interventionist Keynesian approaches to economy and society. Externally, there had been disastrous failures on the international scene with the military fiasco in Vietnam and the continuing menace of communism; the defiance of the OPEC cartel in oil pricing when most Americans thought that the USA was self-sufficient in oil; and the challenge to the USA's Fordist industrial hegemony by Japan and to some extent the European Union. Largely as a result of these affronts to the USA in its position as the bastion of defence against threats to the Western way of life, the New Christian Right enjoyed considerable support during the 1980s. But it has not been so influential during the 1990s, after the collapse of the Soviet Union and the successful, if limited, conclusion of operation Desert Storm in the Gulf War. Although it does not suffer from the same Western cultural prejudice as Islam, the New Christian Right does have in common with it the disadvantage that it is essentially an anti-globalist influence in a world in which secular global influences have not only become firmly established but also in their myriad ways tend to undermine idealistic movements. Moreover, fundamentalism represents a return to tradition and there is an inherent impossibility of achieving this given the essential scepticism (reflexivity) of modernity. Therefore scepticism is both the reason for fundamentalism and the reason for its failure. The USA of the 1980s continued to be the centre of globalized popular culture and it was always unlikely that the New Christian Right would make any inroads into that. In fact the movement's objectives were realistically directed at government institutions like public education and foreign policy. In post-1979 Iran, too, the revitalization of Islamic theology and its application in everyday life has not eradicated Western popular culture, which is found everywhere. As Beyer (1994: 181) puts it: 'in perhaps the greatest irony of the revolution, Islam may have served, not to establish a theocratic rejection of global incorporation, but to rid Iran of its neo-patrimonial heritage and pave the way for a uniquely Iranian particularization of the global universal.' This is a confirmation of interpenetration between the universal and the particular in the re-production of globalization and, for Beyer, the outcome is a form of compromise.

Arjun Appadurai (1990), with the conceptual framework introduced in previous chapters, confronts this by making distinctions in
the incidence and type of global cultural flows. He argues that, 'at all
periods in human history, there have been some disjunctures between the flows of these things, but the sheer speed, scale and volume
of each of these flows is now so great that the disjunctures have
become central to the politics of global culture' (p. 301). More de-
scriptively, he continues, 'The Japanese are notoriously hospitable to
ideas and are stereotyped as inclined to export (all) and import
(some) goods, but they are also notoriously closed to immigration,
like the Swiss, the Swedes and the Saudis.' The suggestion here is that
the notion of global cultural flows can be broken down into different
dimensions and as a result differentials discerned in the interpenetration of the universal and the particular. This is one of the purposes of
Appadurai's fivefold typology. Anthony D. King (1991: 10) describes
this as a contribution to 'the conceptual language which would capture the culture of the capitalist world-economy'. In this, he is influenced by Immanuel Wallerstein's work and appears to regard,
wrongly in my view, the capturing of culture as secondary to that of
the economic structure. However, the suggestion about the nature of
Appadurai's 'scapes' is both clear and useful. Lash and Urry (1994:
307) add to this by stating that Appadurai's five dimensions, 'challenge simple notions of a cultural centre and a subordinate periphery.' Furthermore, the dimensions constitute an attempt at
correspondence with 'the multiple worlds constituted by the historically situated imaginations of persons and groups spread across the
globe. Such worlds are fluid and irregularly shaped.' Lash and Urry
themselves argue that 'mediascapes', the global cultural flows
of electronic communications in all their forms, are eclipsing
'ideoscapes', those of the liberal-democratic state and its competing
ideologies. There are many examples of this, such as the remote
Chinese town with its *karaoke* bar mentioned in chapter 4. The
establishment of a market economy alongside state socialist politics
in China is well known, but the relative power of global electronic
media and state politics is brought out well in this depiction of
provincial life.

We can only speculate about the possible future collapse of state
socialism in China and the Tiananmen Square tragedy of 1989 accentuated this. However, the disembedding of local cultural forms in the
face of global cultural flows and the particularistic reproduction of

global cultural forms may be examined in other cases. That of Japan
has been referred to several times. The familiar characteristics of an
all-enclosing enterprise culture with lifetime employment in Japanese industry are being challenged by younger Japanese who desire
more freedom. This argument is based upon the principle that
Japan's outstanding economic success was a form of face-saving for
defeat in the Second World War, but now the wartime generation is
dead. The test of this theory would be whether the adoption of
Western industrial methods will in the future be accompanied by the
adoption of Western attitudes to work patterns, lifestyles and consumption. But it has already been proposed that in Japan Western
universals have been reproduced in particularistic ways and that this
is part of the explanation for the success of Japan's industrial infrastructure with its characteristic employment patterns and organization forms. For Lash and Urry (1994: 65–81) much attention has
already been given to the study of Japanese industrial relations and
'just-in-time' manufacturing and what interests them more is the
horizontal nature of business organization. To be more precise, it is
the relations between different operational departments or subcontractors, and those between ownership and control which also take
horizontal forms, in contrast to the predominance of vertically hierarchical forms in the West. Moreover, they argue that, since approximately 1973, there has been evidence of less of the direction from
government and banks which was once a defining characteristic of
Japanese industry. This has had the effect of making more space for
information structures in the horizontal organizational forms. As
Lash and Urry (p. 65) put it, 'control is displaced from the verticality
of hierarchical management to market demand at the end of the
production chain'. Within these organizational structures there is a
characteristic Japanese cultural form involving the operation of
groups rather than individuals. This has been reported by Yasusuke
Murakami (1984, 1986: 230) and Michio Morishima (1982, 1991) and
it is here that we might find evidence of a change of attitudes. Peter
Tasker (1987: 113–16) suggests that the outcome is by no means
certain. Certainly the younger generation in Japan now have known
nothing but prosperity and as a result their expectations and demands
are different from those of their parents. These expectations have to
a great extent been derived from television and the global media
and the indications, Tasker believes, are of a generalized lack of
direction. This generation has been dubbed the *shin jinrui*, 'the new

humans', in Japan and this often appears in the news media as a term of censure. During the post-war period of 'economic miracle', Tasker concludes,

> the guiding light has been a special kind of mass pragmatism which has required the sacrifice of individual satisfactions for the economic good of the group. When that is no longer necessary, what is supposed to replace it? No one knows, least of all the new humans, but it is they who must find the answer. (1987: 116)

Bill Emmott (1992: 181–4) also writes of the new humans, noting the disinclination for saving amongst this generation, a further distinction from their parents, and also pointing out that 'the better educated members of this generation are less inclined to stick in the same job for the rest of their life, and more eager to work in smaller, more creative and more entrepreneurial companies' (p. 183). Once again the suggestion is of a move away from the previous emphasis on MITI-directed large corporations and a preference for smaller organizations which actually fit well into the *kanban* structure of integrated service, supply and manufacturing networks. Emmott argues, too, that these trends in social patterns and in work preferences have survived the end of the boom years 1987–90. Although the spending–saving relationship has had to change to some extent, the inclinations are still there and he feels that the long-term outcome will show a decline in the sense of group obligation and an increased desire for personal satisfaction. This would accord in general terms with Giddens's concept of the development of life politics in late modern society and would suggest that it might be applicable to Japanese society as well as to the West, although there are obvious considerations of cultural reproduction to be taken into account. However, attention to life politics will not necessarily undermine *kanban*, since it is now well established in organizational systems that have become heavily invested with electronic technology, particularly in the form of control systems.

Ulf Hannerz (1991) takes the study of global cultural influences and their reproduction in a different direction with consideration of the effects in less developed societies. This may shed light on the resistance of local cultures to global influences. Japan is the prime example of a strongly particularistic culture in which economic power with what Emmott calls 'global reach' has been developed very successfully. By contrast, a less developed country may be considered to have a weaker particularistic culture after years of colonialism and of course less economic power with which to exert influence. Hannerz believes the twentieth century is unique because the world has for the first time ceased to be a 'cultural mosaic'.

> Because of the great increase in the traffic in culture, the large-scale transfer of meaning systems and symbolic forms, the world is increasingly becoming one not only in political and economic terms, as in the climactic period of colonialism, but in terms of its cultural construction as well; a global ecumene of persistent cultural interaction and exchange. This, however, is no egalitarian global village. (1991: 107)

Nevertheless, far from consigning the less developed countries to complete and perpetual domination by the global culture, Hannerz introduces the interesting concept of the 'peripheral corruption scenario'. As he puts it, this is where 'the centre offers its high ideals and its best knowledge, given some institutional form, and where the periphery first adopts them and then soon corrupts them' (p. 108). He takes it to explain amongst other things the tragic distortion of Western institutions that has occurred in many less developed countries. In these cases the representation of the nation-state and of liberal democracy, with all that these entail, becomes a sham. Not only does this represent clear disadvantages for the less developed country but also it gives the core countries of the global culture opportunity to criticize or even denigrate the LDCs' capacity for modernization. On the basis of actual studies in a less developed country, Hannerz goes on to refine these two categories of scenarios. In doing this he accepts that there is a need to build into the concepts adequate dimensions of time and space. The concept of cultural homogenization becomes the 'saturation tendency':

> It would suggest that as the transnational cultural influences, of whatever sort but in large part certainly market organized, and operating in a continuously open structure, unendingly pound on the sensibilities of the people of the periphery, peripheral culture will step by step assimilate more and more of the imported meanings and forms, becoming gradually indistinguishable from the centre. (1991: 122)

The alternative to this is the 'maturation tendency'. The global cultural flows appear at first to be absorbed and reproduced in the local culture. But on further inspection they are not absorbed but merely exist with the local culture in the day-to-day activities of the subject population. With the passage of time, according to Hannerz, the received cultural influences become 'hybridized'. The time dimension is crucial here. In his example of Nigeria, Hannerz points out that European influences have been present in West Africa for several centuries and that twentieth-century global culture is, from the perspective of the local culture, a more powerful version of this. Moreover, what Hannerz calls 'local cultural entrepreneurs' are key actors in the particularization of universals. Given also that localized versions of global culture find their way back to the centre, as in the case of West African rock music for instance, then this is entirely consistent with Robertson's concept of interpenetration between the global and the local.

Jonathan Friedman (1990) advances consideration of the particularization of the universal with his anthropological work on production and consumption amongst peripheral peoples in the context of global culture. His book is based on the premise that production and consumption are more than just material aspects of subsistence, but are constituents of selfhood and social identity. This may be seen as an extension of Hannerz's concept of 'local cultural entrepreneurs'. Friedman uses the example of *la sape* in the People's Republic of the Congo. According to Friedman (p. 315), in full this is *la société des ambianceurs et personnes élégantes*, but it is also associated with 'the verb *se saper* which means the art of dressing elegantly'. The dressing in question is in terms of internationally famous designer names and involves not only expensive imported designer clothes but also sewing on the designer labels externally for immediate recognition. The aim is status – the construction of identity in the periphery, clearly and unmistakably associated with the centre. The acquisition of this identity takes place in the first instance in Brazzaville, as Friedman puts it, the Paris of the Congo, the centre in the periphery – but ultimately Paris itself must be the goal. The participants are undeniably key figures in the local reproduction of globally projected imagery, but they demonstrate conclusively that this is no passive process and that their actions have a bearing on the global nature of the commodity. The universal aspect is in the unquestioning acceptance of the designer label as desirable and the particular aspect is its use as a signifier in the social structure.

Globalization is the tendency for routine day-to-day social interaction to be imbued with patterns that are to an increasing extent shared across the planet. In the transmission of news, television broadcasting enhanced by satellite technology has enabled global instantaneous exchange to be the norm. Supermarkets present a global range of provisions all the year round and so make the produce of the global environment the norm for our subsistence. The nation-state and the nation-state system have rendered citizenship a universal requirement for the legal sanction of human existence: a stateless person does not exist in legal terms. The professionalization of the military and the industrialization of warfare have in combination universalized the nation-state's monopoly of violence and, by default, the definition of counter-measures as terrorism. In all of this, a major question for sociology must be to what extent the techniques and technologies involved have produced not only mass participation on an increasingly global scale but also a real breaking down of gaps between the haves and the have nots. The answer would seem to be that inequalities change with globalization. The emancipation which comes with the individual's reflexive relationship with global institutions brings with it new inequalities or forms of inequality. For instance, in Britain, while unemployment was still at a very high level, 1994 was the first year ever in which more women than men were employed in paid work. Beyond this, on a broader scale, the indications are that it will be people who are conversant with and who keep abreast of developments in electronic technology who will be the haves. The speed of development is accelerating and the have nots will be an underclass of people who are unemployable because of their lack of willingness or ability to keep up with developments. To end on a more optimistic note, John Naisbitt (1994) argues in favour of a paradox inherent in globalization that is a hopeful one: the greater the global whole, the more opportunities there are for the individual.

Bibliography

Abercrombie, Nick, Hill, Stephen and Turner, Bryan 1980: *The Dominant Ideology Thesis*. London: Allen and Unwin.

Abercrombie, Nick, Hill, Stephen and Turner, Bryan (eds) 1990: *Dominant Ideologies*. London: Unwin Hyman.

Abu-Lughod, Janet 1991: Going beyond global babblc. In Anthony D. King (ed.), *Culture, Globalization and the World-System*. London: Macmillan, 131–8.

Albertini, Rudolf von 1982: *Decolonization: the administration and future of the colonies, 1919–1960*. n.p.: Africana.

Albrow, Martin and King, Elizabeth (eds) 1990: *Globalization, Knowledge and Society*. London: Sage in association with the International Sociological Association.

Allen, Robert 1992: *Waste Not, Want Not: the production and dumping of toxic waste*. London: Earthscan.

Appadurai, Arjun 1990: Disjuncture and difference in the global cultural economy. In Mike Featherstone (ed.), *Global Culture: nationalism, globalization and modernity*. London: Sage, 295–310.

Arnason, Johann P. 1990: Nationalism, globalization and modernity. In Mike Featherstone (ed.), *Global Culture: nationalism, globalization and modernity*. London: Sage, 207–36.

Balibar, Etienne 1991: Es gibt keinen Staat in Europa: racism and politics in Europe today. *New Left Review*, 186 (March/April), 5–19.

Barnett, Corelli 1972: *The Collapse of British Power*. New York: William Morrow.

Beck, Ulrich 1988: *Gegengifte: die organisierte Unverantwortlichkeit*. Frankfurt: Suhrkamp.

Beck, Ulrich 1992: *Risk Society: towards a new modernity*. London: Sage in association with *Theory, Culture and Society*.

Beck, Ulrich 1994: The reinvention of politics: towards a theory of reflexive modernization. In Ulrich Beck, Anthony Giddens and Scott Lash, *Reflexive Modernization: politics, tradition and aesthetics in the modern social order*. Cambridge: Polity Press, 1–55.

Beck, Ulrich and Beck-Gernsheim, Elisabeth 1990: *Das ganz normale Chaos der Liebe*. Frankfurt: Suhrkamp. Tr. Mark Ritter and Jane Wieber as *The Normal Chaos of Love*. Cambridge: Polity Press, 1995.

Bendix, Reinhard 1964: *Nation Building and Citizenship*. New York: Wiley.

Berger, Peter, Berger, Brigitte and Kellner, Hansfried 1973: *The Homeless Mind*. New York: Random House.

Beyer, Peter F. 1990: Privatization and the public influence of religion in global society. In Mike Featherstone (ed.), *Global Culture: nationalism, globalization and modernity*. London: Sage, 373–95.

Beyer, Peter 1994: *Religion and Globalization*. London: Sage.

Boli, John. Undated and unpublished research paper: Issues of sovereignty in the world polity: an institutional research agenda. University of Uppsala, Sweden/Stanford University, USA.

Boli, John and Thomas, George M. 1990: *World Culture, World Polity Context of International Non-Governmental Organizations*. Paper submitted to the National Science Foundation.

Braudel, Fernand 1982: *Civilization and Capitalism 15th–18th Century, vol. 2: The Wheels of Commerce*. London: Collins.

Braudel, Fernand 1984: *Civilization and Capitalism 15th–18th Century, vol. 3: The Perspective of the World*. London: Collins.

Budd, Leslie and Whimster, Sam (eds) 1992: *Global Finance and Urban Living: a study of metropolitan change*. London: Routledge.

Burningham, Kate and O'Brien, Martin 1994: Global environmental values and local contexts of action. *Sociology*, 28(4), 913–32.

Cipolla, Carlo M. 1965: *Guns and Sails in the Early Phase of European Expansion 1400–1700*. London: Collins.

Cipolla, Carlo M. 1967: *Clocks and Culture 1300–1700*. New York: Walker.

Cohen, Yehudi 1970: Schools and civilizational systems. In Joseph Fischer (ed.), *The Social Sciences and the Comparative Study of Educational Systems*. Scranton Pa.: International Textbook, 55–147.

Cohen, Yehudi 1979: The state system, schooling, and cognitive and motivational patterns. In Nobuo Shimahara and Adam Scrupski (eds), *Social Forces and Schooling*. New York: McKay, 103–40.

Cowling, Keith and Sugden, Robert 1987: Market exchange and the concept of a transnational corporation. *British Review of Economic Issues*, 9, 57–68.

Crook, Stephen, Pakulski, Jan and Waters, Malcolm 1992: *Postmodernization: change in advanced society*. London: Sage.

Davidson, Basil 1984: *The Story of Africa*. London: Mitchell Beazley.

Davidson, Basil 1994: *Modern Africa: a social and political history*. 3rd edn. London: Longman.

Der Derian, James 1989: The boundaries of knowledge and power in international relations. In James Der Derian and Michael J. Shapiro (eds), *International/Intertextual Relations: postmodern readings of world politics*. Lexington, Mass.: Lexington Books, 3–10.

Dezalay, Yves 1990: The *big bang* and the law: the internationalization and restructuring of the legal field. In Mike Featherstone (ed.), *Global Culture: nationalism, globalization and modernity*. London: Sage, 279–93.

Dicken, Peter 1992: *Global Shift: the internationalization of economic activity*. 2nd edn. London: Paul Chapman.

Dunkerley, David, Spybey, Tony and Thrasher, Michael 1981: Inter-organizational networks: a case study of industrial location. *Organisation Studies*, 2(3), 229–47.

Ekins, Paul 1992: *A New World Order: grass roots movements for social change*. London: Routledge.

Elias, Norbert 1982: *The Civilizing Process, vol. 2: State Formation and Civilization*. Oxford: Basil Blackwell.

Emmott, Bill 1992: *Japan's Global Reach: the influences, strategies and weaknesses of Japan's multinational companies*. London: Century Business.

Esser, Josef 1992: Transnational corporations in a trilateral world. Paper to a symposium of the Andrew Schofield Association, Florence.

Featherstone, Mike (ed.) 1990: *Global Culture: nationalism, globalization and modernity*. London: Sage.

Friedman, Jonathan 1990: Being in the world: globalization and localization. In Mike Featherstone (ed.), *Global Culture: nationalism, globalization and modernity*. London: Sage, 311–28.

Fröbel, Folker, Heinrichs, Jürgen and Kreye, Otto 1980: *The New International Division of Labour* (tr. Peter Burgess). Cambridge: Cambridge University Press.

Fuentes, Annette and Ehrenreich, Barbara 1983: *Women in the Global Factory*. Boston, Mass.: South End Press.

Fukuyama, Francis 1992: *The End of History and the Last Man*. New York: Free Press.

Gamble, Andrew 1990: Britain's decline: some theoretical issues. In Michael Mann (ed.), *The Rise and Decline of the Nation-State*. Oxford: Basil Blackwell, 71–90.

Gamble, Clive 1994: *Timewalkers: the prehistory of global colonization*. London: Alan Sutton.

Gandhi, Mohandas K. (Mahatma) 1909: Letter to H. S. L. Polak (14 October). Included in Raghavan N. Iyer (ed.) 1986: *The Moral and Political Writings of Mahatma Gandhi, vol. 1: Civilization, Politics and Religion*. Oxford: Clarendon Press, 293.

Gayle, Dennis J. 1986: *The Small Developing State: comparing political economies in Costa Rica, Singapore and Jamaica*. Aldershot: Gower.

Gessner, Volkmar and Schade, Angelika 1990: Conflicts of culture in cross-border legal relations: the conception of a research topic in the sociology of law. In Mike Featherstone (ed.), *Global Culture: nationalism, globalization and modernity*. London: Sage, 253–77.

Giddens, Anthony 1984: *The Constitution of Society: outline of the theory of structuration*. Cambridge: Polity Press.

Giddens, Anthony 1985: *The Nation-State and Violence*, vol. 2 of *A Contemporary Critique of Historical Materialism*. Cambridge: Polity Press.

Giddens, Anthony 1990: *The Consequences of Modernity*. Cambridge: Polity Press.

Giddens, Anthony 1991: *Modernity and Self-Identity: self and society in the late modern age*. Cambridge: Polity Press.

Giddens, Anthony 1992: *The Transformation of Intimacy: sexuality, love and eroticism in modern societies*. Cambridge: Polity Press.

Giddens, Anthony 1994: Living in a post-traditional society. In Ulrich Beck, Anthony Giddens and Scott Lash, *Reflexive Modernization: politics, tradition and aesthetics in the modern social order*. Cambridge: Polity Press, 56–109.

Go, Frank M. and Pine, Ray 1995: *Globalization Strategy in the Hotel Industry*. London: Routledge.

Gong, Gerrit W. 1984: *The Standard of 'Civilization' in International Society*. Oxford: Clarendon Press.

Grew, Raymond 1984: The nineteenth century European state. In Charles Bright and Susan Harding (eds), *Statemaking and Social Movements: essays in history and theory*. Ann Arbor: University of Michigan Press, 83–120.

Grun, Bernard 1991: *The Timetables of History: a horizontal linkage of people and events*. 3rd edn. New York: Touchstone.

Hall, John A. 1985: *Powers and Liberties: the causes and consequences of the rise of the West*. Oxford: Basil Blackwell.

Hall, John A. 1994: *Coercion and Consent: studies on the modern state*. Cambridge: Polity Press.

Halliday, Fred 1988: Hidden from international relations: women and the international arena. *Millennium*, 17 (winter), 461.

Hannerz, Ulf 1991: Scenarios for peripheral cultures. In Anthony D. King (ed.), *Culture, Globalization and the World-System*. London: Macmillan, 107–28.

Hebdige, Dick 1990: Fax to the future. *Marxism Today*, January, 18–23.

Hegedüs, Zsuzsa 1990: Social movements and social change in self-creative society: new civil initiatives in the international arena. In Martin Albrow and Elizabeth King (eds), *Globalization, Knowledge and Society*. London: Sage, 263–80.

Held, David 1989: The decline of the nation-state. In Stuart Hall and Martin Jacques (eds), *New Times*. London: Lawrence and Wishart, 191–24.

Henderson, Jeffrey 1989: *The Globalisation of High Technology Production: society, space and semiconductors in the restructuring of the modern world*. London: Routledge.

Herndon, Booton 1970: *Ford: an unconventional biography of the two Henry Fords and their times*. London: Cassell.

Hirst, Paul Q. 1993: Globalisation is fashionable but is it a myth? *Guardian*, 22 March, p. 11.

Hirst, Paul Q. and Thompson, Grahame F. 1992: The problem of 'globalisation': international economic relations, national economic management and the formation of trading blocs. *Economy and Society*, 21(4), 357–96.

Hirst, Paul Q. and Thompson, Grahame F. 1994: Globalization, foreign direct investment and international economic governance. *Organization*, 1(2), 277-303.

Hohenberg, Paul M. and Lees, Lynn Hollen 1985: *The Making of Urban Europe 1000–1950*. Cambridge, Mass.: Harvard University Press.

International Broadcasting Trust 1985: *The People Trade: bargain basements*. London: an International Broadcasting Trust production for Channel Four Television (videocassette).

Kahn, Herman 1979: *World Economic Development: 1979 and beyond*. London: Croom Helm.

Keegan, John 1993: *A History of Warfare*. London: Hutchinson.

Kerr, Clark, Dunlop, John T., Harbison, Frederick and Myers, Charles A. 1960: *Industrialism and Industrial Man*. Cambridge, Mass.: Harvard University Press. 2nd edn (with foreword and postscript), 1973: Harmondsworth: Penguin.

Ketcham, R. 1987: *Individualism and Public Life: a modern dilemma*. Oxford: Basil Blackwell.

King, Anthony D. 1990: *Global Cities: post-imperialism and the internationalization of London*. London: Routledge.

King, Anthony D. 1991a: Introduction: spaces of culture, spaces of knowledge. In Anthony D. King (ed.), *Culture, Globalization and the World-System*. London: Macmillan, 1–18.

King, Anthony D. (ed.) 1991b: *Culture, Globalization and the World-System*. London: Macmillan in association with the Department of Art and Art History, State University of New York at Binghampton.

Lamb, Geoff 1981: Rapid capitalist development models: a new politics of dependence? In Dudley Seers (ed.), *Dependency Theory: a critical reassessment*. London: Frances Pinter, 97–108.

Lash, Scott 1993: Reflexive modernization: the aesthetic dimension. *Theory, Culture and Society*, 10 (1), 1–24.

Lash, Scott 1994: Reflexivity and its doubles: structure, aesthetics, community. In Ulrich Beck, Anthony Giddens and Scott Lash, *Reflexive Modernization: politics, tradition and aesthetics in the modern social order.* Cambridge: Polity Press, 110–73.

Lash, Scott and Urry, John 1987: *The End of Organized Capitalism.* Cambridge: Polity Press.

Lash, Scott and Urry, John 1994: *Economies of Signs and Space.* London: Sage.

Litvinoff, Barnet 1991: *Fourteen Ninety Two: the year and the era.* London: Constable.

Lopez, Robert S. 1963: The crossroad within the wall. In Oscar Handlin and John Burchard (eds), *The Historian and the City.* Cambridge, Mass.: MIT Press, 27–43.

Luhmann, Niklas 1971: Die Weltgesellschaft. *Archiv für Rechts- und Sozialphilosophie*, 57, 1–35.

Luhmann, Niklas 1982: *The Differentiation of Society.* New York: Columbia University Press.

Lukes, Steven 1977: *Essays in Social Theory.* London: Macmillan.

Lyotard, Jean-François 1984: *The Postmodern Condition: a report on knowledge.* Manchester: Manchester University Press.

MacCannell, Dean 1976: *The Tourist: a new theory of the leisure class.* London: Macmillan.

MacCannell, Dean 1992: *Empty Meeting Grounds: tourist papers.* London: Routledge.

McNeill, William H. 1982: *The Pursuit of Power: technology, armed force and society since AD 1000.* Oxford: Basil Blackwell.

McNeill, William H. 1985: *Polyethnicity and National Unity in World History.* Toronto: University of Toronto Press.

Mann, Michael 1986: *The Sources of Social Power, vol. 1: A History of Power from the Beginning to AD 1760.* Cambridge: Cambridge University Press.

Mann, Michael 1990: Introduction: empires with ends. In Michael Mann (ed.), *The Rise and Decline of the Nation-State.* Oxford: Basil Blackwell, 1–11.

Mann, Michael 1993: *The Sources of Social Power, vol. 2: The Rise of Classes and Nation-States, 1760–1914.* Cambridge: Cambridge University Press.

Meier, Artur 1990: The peace movement: some questions concerning its social nature and structure. In Martin Albrow and Elizabeth King (eds), *Globalization, Knowledge and Society.* London: Sage, 251–61.

Mitter, Swasti 1986: *Common Fate, Common Bond: women in the global economy.* London: Pluto Press.

Morgan, D. 1979: *Merchants of Grain.* New York: Viking Press.

Morishima, Michio 1982: *Why has Japan 'Succeeded'?* Cambridge: Cambridge University Press.

Morishima, Michio 1991: Information sharing and firm performance in Japan. *Industrial Relations*, 30, 37–61.

Murakami, Yasusuke 1984: *Ie* society as a pattern of civilization. *Journal of Japanese Studies*, 10(2), 281–363.

Murakami, Yasusuke 1986: Technology in transition: two perspectives on industrial policy. In Patrick H. (ed.), *Japan's High Technology Industries: lessons and limitations of industrial policy*. Seattle: University of Washington Press, 211–41.

Naisbitt, John 1994: *Global Paradox*. London: Nicholas Brearley Publishing.

Offe, Claus 1985: *Disorganized Capitalism*. Cambridge: Polity Press.

Ohmae, Kenichi 1985: *Triad Power: the coming shape of global competition*. New York: Free Press.

Ohmae, Kenichi 1990: *The Borderless World*. London: Collins.

Oman, Charles 1994: *Globalization and Regionalization: the challenge for developing countries*. Paris: OECD Development Centre.

Palloix, Christian 1975: The internationalization of capital and the circuit of social capital. In Hugo Radice (ed.), *International Firms and Modern Imperialism*. Harmondsworth: Penguin, 63–88.

Palloix, Christian 1977: The self-expansion of capital on a world scale. *Review of Radical Political Economics*, 9, 1–28.

Parkin, Frank 1971: *Class Inequality and the Political Order: social stratification in capitalist and communist countries*. London: MacGibbon and Kee.

Peterson, Spike V. and Runyan, Anne Sisson 1993: *Global Gender Issues*. Boulder, Colo.: Westview Press.

Phizacklea, Annie 1990: *Unpacking the Fashion Industry: gender, racism and class in production*. London: Routledge & Kegan Paul.

Porritt, Jonathon 1988: Greens and growth. *UK Campaign for Environmental Economic Development Bulletin*, 19, 22–3.

Princen, Thomas and Finger, Matthias, with Clark, Margaret L. and Manno, Jack 1994: *Environmental NGOs in World Politics: linking the local and the global*. London: Routledge.

Ramirez, Francisco O. and Boli, John 1987: The political construction of mass schooling: European origins and worldwide institutionalization. *Sociology of Education*, 60(1), 2–17.

Redclift, Michael and Benton, Ted (eds) 1994: *Social Theory and the Global Environment*. London: Routledge.

Reisner, Edward 1922: *Nationalism and Education since 1789*. New York: Macmillan.

Ringer, Fritz K. 1977: *Education and Society in Modern Europe*. Bloomington, Ind.: Indiana University Press.

Ritzer, George 1993: *The McDonaldization of Society: an investigation into the changing character of social life*. Thousand Oaks, Ca.: Pineforge Press.

Roberts, John M. 1985: *The Triumph of the West*. London: BBC Publications.

Roberts, John M. 1992: *History of the World*. London: Helicon.

Robertson, Roland 1992: *Globalization: social theory and global culture*. London: Sage.

Robinson, Jeffrey 1994: *The Laundrymen: inside the world's third largest business*. London: Simon and Schuster.

Roche, Maurice 1992: *Rethinking Citizenship: welfare, ideology and change in modern society*. Cambridge: Polity Press.

Rosecrance, Richard 1986: *The Rise of the Trading State: commerce and conquest in the modern world*. New York: Basic Books.

Ross, Dorothy 1991: *The Origins of American Social Science*. Cambridge: Cambridge University Press.

Scarfi, Tony 1992: Towards a global language. *Guardian Education*, 11 February, 4–5.

Scholte, Jan Aart 1993: *International Relations of Social Change*. Buckingham: Open University Press.

Servan-Schreiber, Jean-Jacques 1968: *The American Challenge*. London: Hamish Hamilton.

Shaw, Martin 1991: *Post-Military Society: militarism, demilitarization and war at the end of the twentieth century*. Cambridge: Polity Press.

Shaw, Martin 1994: *Global Society and International Relations: sociological concepts and political perspectives*. Cambridge: Polity Press.

Siegenthaler, U. and Oeschger, H. 1987: Biospheric carbon dioxide emissions during the past 200 years by deconvolution of the ice core data. *Tellus*, 39b, 140–54.

Sklair, Leslie 1994: Global sociology and global environmental change. In Michael Redclift and Ted Benton (eds), *Social Theory and Global Environment*. London: Routledge, 205–27.

Smith, Alan K. 1991: *Creating a World Economy: merchant capital, colonialism and world trade, 1400–1825*. Boulder, Colo.: Westview Press.

Smith, Anthony D. 1979: *Nationalism in the Twentieth Century*. New York: New York University Press.

Smith, Anthony D. 1992: National identity and the idea of European unity. *International Affairs*, 68(1), 55–76.

Smith, Michael Peter (ed.) 1992: *After Modernism: global restructuring and the changing boundaries of city life*. New Brunswick, NJ: Transaction Publishers.

Spybey, Tony 1982: The rationality of the business organization in advanced capitalist society. University of Bradford: Ph.D. thesis.

Spybey, Tony 1984: Traditional and professional frames of meaning for managers. *Sociology*, 18(4), 550–62.

Spybey, Tony 1992: *Social Change, Development and Dependency: modernity, colonialism and the rise of the West*. Cambridge: Polity Press.

Tasker, Peter 1987: *Inside Japan: wealth, work and power in the new Japanese empire*. Harmondsworth: Penguin.

Tenbruck, Friedrich H. 1990: The dream of a secular ecumene: the meaning and limits of policies of development. In Mike Featherstone (ed.), *Global Culture: nationalism, globalization and modernity*. London: Sage, 193–206.

Thubron, Colin 1989: *The Silk Road China: beyond the celestial kingdom*. London: Pyramid Books.

Touraine, Alain 1981: *The Voice and the Eye*. Cambridge: Cambridge University Press.

Turner, Bryan S. 1990: The two faces of sociology: global or national? In Mike Featherstone (ed.), *Global Culture: nationalism, globalization and modernity*. London: Sage, 343–58.

Turner, Bryan S. 1994: *Orientalism, Postmodernism and Globalism*. London: Routledge.

Urry, John 1990: *The Tourist Gaze*. London: Sage.

Wagner, Peter 1994: *A Sociology of Modernity: liberty and discipline*. London: Routledge.

Wallerstein, Immanuel 1979: *The Capitalist World-Economy*. Cambridge: Cambridge University Press.

Wallerstein, Immanuel 1982: Crisis as transition. In Samir Amin, Giovanni Arrighi, André Gunder Frank and Immanuel Wallerstein, *Dynamics of Global Crisis*. London: Macmillan, 11–54.

Wallerstein, Immanuel 1984: *The Politics of the World-Economy: the states, the movements and the civilizations*. Cambridge: Cambridge University Press.

Weiner, Martin J. 1981: *English Culture and the Decline of the Industrial Spirit 1850–1980*. Cambridge: Cambridge University Press.

Woods, Bernard 1993: *Communication, Technology and the Development of People*. London: Routledge.

World Bank 1994: *World Development Report 1994: infrastructure for development*. Oxford: Oxford University Press.

Worsley, Peter 1984: *The Three Worlds: culture and world development*. London: Weidenfeld and Nicolson.

Wu, Yuan-Li 1985: *Becoming an Industrialized Nation: ROC's development on Taiwan*. New York: Praeger.

Yearley, Steven 1994: Social movements and environmental change. In Michael Redclift and Ted Benton (eds), *Social Theory and Global Environment*. London: Routledge, 150–68.

Zerubavel, E. 1981: *Hidden Rhythms: schedules and calendars in social life*. Chicago, Ill.: University of Chicago Press.

Zhao, Ding-Xin and Hall, John A. 1994: State power and patterns of late development: resolving the crisis of the sociology of development. *Sociology*, 28(1), 211–29.

Zukin, Sharon 1992: The city as a landscape of power. London and New York as global financial capitals. In Leslie Budd and Sam Whimster (eds), *Global Finance and Urban Living: a study of metropolitan change.* London: Routledge, 195–223.

Index